MOM BOSS

BALANCING ENTREPRENEURSHIP, KIDS & SUCCESS

Nicole Feliciano founder *of* **MomTrends**

ISBN 978-1-63353-394-3

*I just love bossy women.
I could be around them all day. To me,
bossy is not a pejorative term at all.
It means somebody's passionate and
engaged and ambitious and doesn't
mind leading.*

– Amy Poehler

To C & S, may you grow up to be bossy.

TABLE OF CONTENTS

FOREWORD

There's a popular notion out there that the height of being a modern woman is to achieve the perfect balance between all of life's big-bucket categories. We hear the idea "work/life balance" so often we don't stop to recognize that the inherent insinuation in that phrase is that work is somehow separate from life or even the opposite of it. We keep hearing we can "have it all," "do it all," and "be it all"—and although none of us have ever personally experienced this balancing act first hand, maybe we keep repeating it, hoping if we say it enough times, we will summons the concept into existence.

But I believe the real mark of being a modern woman is to know that everything costs something...and then to confidently decide which costs we're willing to pay—and which we aren't.

When I first met Nicole Feliciano over breakfast in Los Angeles, she described this experience: "We have these burners all going at the same time...family, romance, career, friends...and we try so hard to keep them all going at once. But the reality is something always seems to be burning, but there are other things coming out perfectly."

Maybe the truth is, we can have it all...just not all at once. And that's good news. The life of a mother is filled with stages that demand imbalance—times when we need to turn up the heat on some areas in our life and turn it down in others in order to be the type of moms we want to be. Continuous balance in all areas is hardly ever what we really want.

Nicole went on, "At some point, each of those things are going to win and each one will lose. You have to embrace that you can only do a few things really well at one particular time." An authentic voice of experience I could relate to.

I had also learned that being a mom and a businesswoman can have high costs. I spent my 20's and 30's in traditional career mode, first working on the floor of the Chicago Mercantile Exchange, then working in finance, and then traveling the world as a business consultant. Somewhere in there I managed to get married and have a daughter. My husband would pick me up from the airport each Friday and drop me back off every Sunday afternoon; I would kiss my sweet daughter in her car seat, and wave goodbye, giving the biggest smile I could muster, when really I felt sick to my stomach. I was not the mom I had always hoped to be.

And so I quit. I needed to be with my family. But not working wasn't the answer. I felt there just had to be opportunities out there where a woman could have more control, making deliberate tradeoffs as it made sense for her family. Not finding what I was after in the marketplace, I became determined to create an opportunity for all the women who were just like me, feeling the immense tension and feelings of guilt that come with having to constantly choose career or family. Most women I knew wanted both, in varying degrees.

With a fervor to create a solution, I gathered with a group of friends from variousbackgrounds to create an opportunity where a woman could have her own business— totally on her own terms, her own schedule, and her own desired paycheck. But we didn't want to create just any job—we wanted this opportunity to be something truly meaningful, that would fill up a woman's heart, giving her the deep relational bonds that bring a unique richness to life. In partnership with a talented and established clothing designer, we created "cabi," a company through which women could become fashion stylists, holding trunk shows with groups of friends, then working with each woman to help her discover her personal style and maximize her wardrobe.

Clothing is not only a product always in demand, but time spent with women developing authentic relationship is in high demand too in our increasingly frenetic world.

Over the last 15 years, we have experienced strong and steady growth—all because our Stylists have experienced the same as they live fulfilling lives as their own bosses. The moments my heart has most overflowed over the last decade and a half are when I hear women, often moms, share with me why their experience with cabi has transformed their life, bringing to it a quality they had no idea they so desperately needed. I hear from women who'd been working a corporate grind that kept them from being a part of their kids' most important milestones, but their income through cabi enabled them to quit and be the homeroom mom and the leader of the cheering section on the lacrosse field. I love the stories of moms who had made a decision to stay home with little ones, but find they had lost a part of themselves that has been regained and elevated through running their own cabi businesses. Our 85% retention each season fills me with profound joy, because it's evidence our business really works and the stories I hear over and over reinforce the profound liberation that can be had for a woman in charge of the heat under each of her burners.

Upon meeting Nicole, we were quickly on the same page with many common passions and draw-a-line-in-the-sand moments. We both had waded through our deep longings to bring our God given brains and talents to a bigger arena, but also wanted to give our unfettered hearts and minds to those we love most. But we connected most deeply on our common desire not just to attain this for ourselves, but to help other women to do the same. This seems to be the space where life has yielded the most fulfillment for both of us.

Nicole's story is readily seen as one of courage and tenacity. But, much deeper than that, hers is a story of discernment and integrity. And I think it's actually pretty ironic that a woman devoted to trends would be so steadfast in not following so many of them. And thank goodness. As other bloggers seek to make themselves a celebrity, Nicole seeks to make those she serves the hero. When other media companies are willing to endorse anything when top-dollar is offered, Nicole has turned down huge deals to stay true to her ideals. She knows what she believes and what she's about. And she so graciously shares her wisdom and lessons of experience with others to their benefit.

Nicole, and by extension MomTrends, is that wise person you can't get enough of in your life. She's the friend who has the gift of bringing value, thoughtfulness, and realness. She has great taste and a commitment to quality, keeping the bar high for herself and others. She puts relationships first—in her business, at home, and with friends. She endeavors to be fully present wherever she is, eager to contribute the best= of herself for the sake of others. Her audience – 100,000⁺ people strong—comes back regularly because she and her colleagues give them insights about the things that really matter to them.

So if you're trying to figure out how you could possibly become a Mom Boss with all the demands that encircle you, or if you've been dreaming from time to time and just looking for that last ounce of gumption to launch your own thing, or if you've ventured into the world of business building and been burned, you're in good hands. Nicole will help you muster the confidence to try (or try again). She'll give you all the right things to think about to get headed on the right path toward a life of calling your own shots. She's not only lived and breathed the uncertainty of leaving the safety of a steady paycheck for the reward of forging your own way, but she also surrounds herself with women who have done the same. She senses into the felt needs of the thousands of women who are part of the MomTrends community, making her a true authority on what the modern mom most deeply desires and how to get there.

Ready to have "work" and "life" no longer in opposition?

You're in the right place.

Kimberly Inskeep
President of Cabi

CHAPTER 1

MOM BOSS

Here's how it played out. Stephanie worked for luxury beauty brands for more than a decade. Being a dutiful Gen X feminist, Stephanie returned to work after her 6-month maternity leave (the last three months unpaid) for both baby number one and number two.

The scene with one child and work was pretty manageable. The second child stretched her resources thin. Stephanie skulked out of meetings to go pump breast milk in a dimly lit back office and stashed her bags of milk in the community fridge, before heading to the next meeting apologetically late.

She drafted emails to her team and CEO explaining her challenging schedule for the week: Monday she needed to visit a preschool for an interview at 3pm, and Thursday she needed to take her son to the pediatric ophthalmologist at 1:50pm (the only appointment available all month). She felt she earned the right to be unavailable, but that didn't make it any easier.

When Stephanie was blessed with her third child, she never returns after maternity leave. Juggling the third and having to start apologizing again for being the type of mom she wanted to be didn't hold any appeal.

With some savings tucked away, she droped out for a bit.l Then, she gets a niggling idea that there should be an in-home service for teaching moms how to prep homemade baby food. The idea was to develop a weeklong course that empowered women to create DIY baby food and stock the fridge with homemade goodness. After informal focus groups with her friends, she fine-tuned the idea and started a baby chef business plan. She could now work around her family's schedule and market within her built-in network. Six months after launching, she had clients on a waitlist to use her service and a growing brand she loved.

This story is a conglomeration of three of my friends, and I bet it'll sound really familiar to some of you. I bet you know a mom who's done something similar and is living her dream. A dream she didn't even know she had before the kids came along.

Kids have a funny way of changing your dreams. Prepping for your first child is such a strange practice. It's all about cogitating variables with little or no information. It's hard to say how you'll feel after your baby arrives, or what kind of baby you're going to get. For most of us, there's a surge of love and protectiveness. We can't imagine putting anyone else in charge. After waiting 30+ years to find the right person to start a family, or find the time and money to be a single mom, we want to fully embrace the experience.

But the reality of raising a family is that it's expensive. Someone has to pay for diapers and doctor visits. So work we must;. Millennial moms have the right idea. Stories of their unwillingness to compromise and take a job that's ok instead of awesome are the first step to owning an incredible future. Gen X and Gen Y mom are catching up with this savvy crew, and adopting this attitude of "it has to work for me."

We can all take a page from managing our post-kid careers with this attitude; sheepishly having to ask a boss or co-workers for permission to be a great mom stinks. In our hearts, we know we can give our family the best and still deliver a great presentation, or a fantastic sales plan. We just need options. The trouble is, most workplaces aren't structured for motherhood.

The good news is you can create a career that works for you. That's what being a Mom Boss is all about; it all starts with getting out your stroller and heading to the playground.

Playgrounds are ripe with promise and networking opportunities. That's where I hatched my business plans and started to dream big about my future company. With one eye on my daughter's progress digging and re-digging trenches in a sand pit, my mind wandered to what was next. Finding work that allowed me to be incredibly engaged with my family and financially successful… that was my end goal. It wasn't a company or brand I longed to work for, it was myself.

I'm lucky to live in a city that supports female startups. In New York City, 21 percent of all startups are women-run. That's well ahead of the national average *3. Zoom in even more on Google maps to my borough in NYC, and things get even more interesting. Brooklyn is blessed with the highest percentage of female CEOs in the nation. Where I live, 28 percent of startups are female-led. No wonder I love Brooklyn so much!

When I settled in to Brooklyn over a decade ago, it had an indie vibe to it; the parents I met wanted to do things on their own terms. All this energy of acceptance and possibility rubbed off on me. At first, I thought it was just a Brooklyn thing. Visit any Brooklyn playground and you're likely to be surrounded by women who are passionate about raising children (I know the sitcoms sure like to make fun of our earnest efforts to recycle and raise self-advocating kids!). The Brooklyn parks also happen to be populated with talented, educated, savvy businesswomen brimming with possibility.

Living where I do, surrounded by female awesomeness and risk-takers, at first I felt like I was in a little bubble. I thought the self-selecting group of moms in my tribe was rare. Our neighborhood seemed to be full of women who were drawn to Brooklyn's slightly less Type-A feel. The focus wasn't so much on accumulating wealth and status, as it was on carving out an authentically happy life. Why are we in a playground and not a boardroom or corner office? My peers are unwilling to compromise family for the traditional trappings of success and how families should operate.

Turns it's not just a Brooklyn thing and it's not just a NYC thing. As I started to get deeper into the digital community and my network expanded, I identified Mom Bosses everywhere. Mom Boss hotbeds are popping up in Utah, Silicon Valley, and Washington D.C. - all hubs of creative energy and mom entrepreneurs. The movement is spreading, and it's time to share the secret sauce - time to encourage more women to take the leap.

The more I talk to women and interact with them on my social media accounts, the more I hear the cries of, "I want this too!" Moms across the country, and around the world, are conflicted and constrained by work/life issues.

MBAs, JDs, women who managed millions of dollars in sales or hundreds of employees, continue to step off a traditional career path to raise a family. Sure, modern parents are figuring out ways to split the workload and shift our priorities, but let's be realistic: while modern parenting is certainly becoming more equitable, women still are far and away the primary caregivers when it comes to raising kids. And that's not even taking into account all the single mothers who don't even have and option of picking who stays home to watch baby, and who gets to work. They have to pick BOTH.

The pressure to work and raise children isn't just about answering the question of who's the lead parent. It's also a question of whose career can take a hit. Many of my peers decided that since they were on a path to have multiple kids, the on-again off-again schedule of pregnancy and maternity leave left them feeling like there wasn't a path for them.

Less than 5 percent of women hold Fortune 500 CEO roles[1]. Things aren't any better in the ranks of top law firms. Raise your hand if you worked at one of these places and are surprised.

Anyone? Anyone? No, I didn't think so. If you're a mom, you likely know why: Asking for permission to breastfeed, or to attend a pre-school interview, or an appointment with one of the myriad of specialists children need to see is degrading and disheartening. Mom Bosses don't ask for time off, they know they've earned it. Reclaiming how and where you spend your precious time is an incredible gift.

LeanIn.org tells us 43 percent of highly qualified women with children are leaving careers or off-ramping for a period of time."[2] I bow to the 57 percent of my friends who are doing it all in a structured environment – Momtrends was started to support them. We develop content for women without the time and energy to stay up to speed on the latest trends. Momtrends.com is predominantly read by working moms. Our team strives to curate the best of the best for them. I want my sisters busting the glass ceiling to success as much as anyone else. Here's to systemic change for women!

In the meantime, I want to make sure that talented moms know they've got options.

Mom Boss life is for the 43 percent of women who are like me. They are smart, qualified, and ready to work hard. If companies won't change, the women running them will. We know that women are incredibly adept at change. Show me any woman with young kids, and I'll show you someone that knows how to handle a curveball! Heck, we can change our bodies into baby-carrying vessels, a new job is nothing!

Plan A is change the system. More power to the women doing that. Plan B is make a new system. That's where Mom Bosses are placing bets.

"WHEN OPPORTUNITY DOESN'T PRESENT ITSELF, IT'S TIME TO MAKE YOUR OWN LUCK."

Why the rise of the Mom Boss? Because businesses aren't changing quickly enough. Moms are taking their talents and finding a new playing field; a field where merit and smarts matter more than office politics and posturing.

Turns out we're really good at being bosses. We've always been amazing at building communities, support networks, and, of course, families.

It's no surprise we're also good at running businesses. We share, build, create, and work really, really hard.

Don't fear the unknown too much. We've got this. We already know how to build a network, prioritize, and set goals. Look at what we've already achieved. In addition to growing babies, we care for sick relatives, manage the house, and somehow find time to keep up on the latest tech. In my house, I'm the head of IT as well as the "cruise director" when it comes to our social lives. I know my girls' BFFs and make sure our house rarely runs out of toilet paper.

IN ESSENCE, EVERY NEW MOM IS ALREADY RUNNING A STARTUP CORPORATION.

Think about all the new things we had to learn and set up after the baby arrived. Each week demanded we master a new skill set. As a new mom, failure was NOT an option. Don't say you can't handle HR if you've already managed to find a good pediatrician that can always squeeze you in for a reoccurring ear infection, or scored a reliable baby sitter who also cleans up after she serves the kids dinner.

We've also figured out how to master budgeting and time management. The worries of a startup are insignificant hurdles in the face of everything we've already learned to do well. Congratulations! As a mom, you've already successfully created your first startup. Being a Mom Boss won't be much different.

And there's more good news. This book is full of examples of women who are blazing paths that work with raising kids. While being self-employed isn't for everyone, it's an increasingly appealing option. It all felt anecdotal when I started thinking about this book. I knew lots of women in the social media space who started blogs a decade agony to earn a little money and get the creative juices flowing. These blogs turned into media corporations and million-dollar businesses like mine. As I started networking, all different types of Mom Bosses presented themselves. From Etsy shops, to at-home sales representatives, to accountants, I kept meeting inspiring moms working towards their dreams while raising families.

These Mom Bosses don't have to ask for permission to coach a soccer league, run a Girl Scout troupe, or drive to a band practice.

Ladies, its tome to makes your own schedule and your own rules. Is the time right for you?

Maybe you've got a burning desire to finally bring an invention to life. Or maybe you want to put your sales acumen to work from home so you don't have to suffer through one more week of your commute. Maybe you've got a child with special needs and simply can't get in to an office anymore. For all these reasons and a million more, Mom Boss life is beckoning. Get ready for the ride!

Warning: You'll be head of IT, HR, and maintenance. The buck stops with you. As I'm writing this, I'm setting on a stressful cash crunch. A few of our accounts are overdue by three months. Collection calls emails are just part of the job. But here's the thing: I'm writing and emailing from a ski lodge in New Hampshire. I was able to leave my Brooklyn office for five days to take my daughter to an East Coast alpine championship ski race. No one had to give me permission to take time off.

As I tucked my pint-sized skier into bed the night before the race, she gave me a huge hug and said, "You're the best mommy every, thank you so, so, so much for taking me here. My heart is fhll. I love you mommy." Cue the tears. Those moments when you melt, you just know the sacrifices are worth it all. I can be a CEO and I can be a "Ski Mom." I'm most definitely a Mom Boss.

NOTES

Chapter 2

MOM GUILT

Mom guilt is real. It's a force that can be used for good or for evil. Let me explain."Are you traveling again?" Working moms across the nation have heard this lament when the kiddos see the roller bag out on the bed. What the mom hears is, "Don't you love me?"

That's not really what the kids are saying. What they are saying is: how is this trip going to affect me? The trick to avoiding mom guilt is to know in your own mind why you are working and what motivates you to work. From talking to friends and from my own experience, you can tame 80 percent of guilt if you are working smart and have a clear goal t o share.

Don't be fooled into thinking that 20 percent of the time mom guilt just stinks, and can't be rationalized away. Work to manage the 80 percent, and then have good friends and family to get you through the 20 percent (and I've got a few tips on how to recover after those brutal 90-hour work weeks, or back-to-back business trips that result in bitter spouses and weepy children).

This was the recent chorus that awaited me at the family dinner table. Mr. Momtrends and I were busy mapping out our travel schedules. My girls were used to his travel. As an investment professional, he often traveled to research companies or do marketing presentations. Life went on smoothly when my husband had a business trip. Since he was not the one coordinating kid schedules, not much changed when we was on the road. Life was a lot less fun, but the show went on.

Not so much for me.

Turns out, I'm the only one who remembers my older daughter likes honey mustard on her sandwiches and won't eat ham, while the younger one likes mayonnaise and prefers ham to turkey. I also know that the piano teacher prefers to be paid in cash, not by check, and that we need to order a new chess clock for an upcoming tournament.

THE DELICIOUS MINUTIAE OF MOTHERHOOD LIVE IN MY HEAD.

I left the corporate world for all these reasons. I wanted to be in charge of the details. I wanted my girls to know that they could count on me. I wanted to be the mom that wouldn't miss a recital or Greek play at school because of an ogre boss. Now I'm the boss, and I have to make these tough calls and prioritize.

As my business has grown, my husband has picked up a lot of the parenting slack - especially when it comes to business travel. But he has his own style (I can't touch the smoothie bar he operates in the morning out of our kitchen), and he most certainly isn't on top of all the child-related things I cover. And he can't braid hair. Oh, and the outfits, well, let's just say the girls don't always look Instagram ready. But he loves them fiercely, has his own rituals, and always gets them to school on time. The mom guilt comes in because he doesn't do it my way.

Each work trip I make requires not just the travel planning, but also the home planning. This is my major source of mom guilt. I make color-coded calendars, send endless emails, and rely on friends and family to pitch in. Still, the nagging feeling that I'm not doing enough remains.

On my most recent trip, I got on the phone with my eight-year-old. She was quite upset with me. Apparently, no one told her I was heading to Utah to work on our Digital Family Ski Guide. The work trip fell at a horrible time for her. It was right after a trip to New Hampshire with my older daughter. I took time off of work to take daughter #1 to a championship ski race on the East Coast. Chalk one up in the "good mom" category, I thought. Nope. Daughter #2 felt slighted, and then horrified, that as soon as I got back from New Hampshire I re-packed and headed off again.

I made headway with the little one over a few phone calls, and assured her that on the next trip, I would give her ample warning of where I was going, and when it was all happening. Crisis averted.

Until I got the text from my husband from the urgent care facility in Brooklyn: broken toe for the older daughter. Sometimes, you just can't win.

What you can do, is manage the fallout.

I'm not alone. Jyl Pattee, founder of Mom It Forward Media, has mastered handling the fall out of business travel. Mom It Forward Media is a boutique digital agency that does many cool things –including producing an annual retreat in partnership with Universal Orlando Resort focused on "creating superhero families." She lives in Utah. You guessed it, her work involves travel.

Part of the reason Jyl founded Mom It Forward, was to make the key milestones in her kids' lives. She used to beat heself up that she worked outside the home and traveled a lot when her kids were in the potty training years.

Now Jyl's boys are teens, and the good news is Jyl reports that Mom Guilt eases as the kids get older. Plus, she's wiser. "I have much more realistic expectations, and am much gentler on myself now," Jyl says. "I let others help, and I share the load with my husband."

Maybe we don't need to be super moms. On most days, just showing up with all your heart counts for a ton.

Business travel is just one source of guilt. No matter how many hours you spend on your business, any toddler will tell you it's too much, and that there should be less work and more tea parties or snuggles.

Good point. Let's talk about balance and ways to find where to fit in the snuggles with the spreadsheets.

FOMO No More

I know some many women who suffer from the mom version of FOMO (Fear of Missing Out). We want to have all the juicy assignments at work AND be superstar moms. It rarely works that way. There is absolutely no use in comparing your situation to others; no one is doing it perfectly. Well, those that are probably wouldn't be fun to have as friends, anyhow. Remember: Comparison is the thief of joy. I, for one, have not actually baked anything for a bake sale in ten years. I write a check and volunteer for almost every field trip. Spending hours in the kitchen without my kids, working on a cake, just doesn't make sense for me.

Flip the Guilt

Give your kids examples of things you turned down to be with them. I'm not telling you to become a martyr; I do want you to be honest. I was recently invited to Sweden to test drive a new Volvo model. As a brand fan, I thought the opportunity was amazing. As a business owner, I saw it as an opportunity to secure some new marketing dollars. Trouble is, the trip was planned over summer break, and we didn't have childcare coverage. The trip overlapped with some down time I planned to spend with the girls, and Mr. Momtrends already had a business trip planned. It was a great life lesson for everyone. I said no to the trip and explained why to my girls. I told them they mattered more than the new business connection. I knew it was the right call for my family. The epic amount of work it would have taken to pull off childcare, plus the disappointment of the girls, made it a clear "no." My ambitious side had to curl up and throw myself a little pity party, but it was a win for family time.

Explain Why Your Work Matters

One of the "aha" moments I've had while building my brand occurred a few years ago. The girls were young and didn't have full-time school yet. I worked around their pre-K schedules during the day, and then put in several hours at night after they went to bed. Mr. Momtrends called me out on my erratic schedule and asked me why I was working so hard. The answer was two-fold: To make myself proud, and to make the girls proud. It was 100 percent the right answer. Having two young girls witness the ups and downs of being a Mom Boss is awesome. I don't want them to think it's easy, or that success doesn't come with sacrifices. I say no to things all the time, because I have very clear priorities. I tell my girls that thanks to my hard work, I am employing nine other moms. Moms who can have careers that allow them to see THEIR children's soccer games and school plays. While they don't always appreciate the big picture, they are slowing grasping my role in the financial ecosystem.

Play Among Peers

Swapping "Mom Fail" stories like the broken toe are essential to my mental health. Thankfully, I have a great group of friend to share laughs; hearing how fellow moms are coping usually does the trick to make me feel better. Not only do I adore the work ethic of my team at Momtrends, I also love how honest they are about working mom life. Knowing that you aren't alone, and that the struggle is real, goes a long way towards alleviating Mom Guilt.

It's easy to get wrapped up in work projects. When you're starting out, there might not be funds to pay for a babysitter to find time to build your business. There are two schools of thought: invest some capital into the business so you can hire help, or start with what you have, and scale up as more money and time gets freed up.

Develop a Schedule

Realistically, running a startup means you've got to be flexible and ready to dive deep; that doesn't mean you can't set up goal hours for yourself. Letting the kids and your life partners know what to ex-pect can go a long way towards curbing resentment. Remember to ask for help. More and more fathers, co-parents, and grandparents are pitching in to help moms manage their role as CEO.

In Jyl's family, her husband handles the carpooling, homework, and dinners. When she's in town, her boys' routine largely stays the same as when she's traveling. Jyl says, "While owning my own business takes me away from my family due to travel, it also affords me a lot of flexibility when I'm in town." When she's home, she'll regularly take Wednesdays off to attend her son's track meet from 3-6 p.m. This was something she could rarely do when she was working at a nine-to-five job. By sharing a schedule with your family, you can let your children know that someone is always there for them.

The goal is to create as much consistency as possible, and foster a stable environment for your kids. In my world, I take off most Monday and Friday afternoons to pick the girls up at school. In return, I work late on those nights after everyone else goes to bed at night.

Build in Rituals That Make Your Mom Boss Status Fun

Maybe it's pizza night on the day you work late, or you bring home souvenirs from every trip you make. In my case, everyone comes to pick me up from the airport, and I always bring home souvenirs.

Mom Guilt. It's real, and it's powerful. The trick is to harness the passion you have for loving your kids into a force of creativity, and a reason to work hard.

Jyl shared some great wisdom with me about Mom Guilt: "I think guilt is only useful if we, as moms, use it to change and grow. No mother is perfect. We're all a work in progress. If we guilt ourselves into thinking we are not good moms, or less than other moms, that's crossing the line into shame. Shame leads to negative thoughts, and can create a downward spiral of negative behaviors. Recognizing our weaknesses and turning them into strengths helps us become super moms. We could all use that refining!

Don't become a slave to your ambition. Once you start drinking from the nectar of being self-employed, it's pretty intoxicating. There are loads of things to do, and rarely a team to delegate too. Startups can take a lot of your mental and physical energy. Don't forget why you started this in the first place; kids are the reason you pivoted in your career to begin with. Becoming a Mom Boss who works 24/7 isn't the goal. Mom Guilt can at times be a be healthy reminder to check where you are allocating your time and energy.

Ultimately, it's up to you to tame the tiger of guilt. Julie Cole, one of the Founders of Mabel's Labels, puts it like this, "Don't obsess over what people think. Don't beat yourself up if the kids have hot dogs for dinner twice in a row. All these things don't matter. Leave guilt at the door. It's a waste of time. What matters is that you forge ahead, get down to work, and live your passion. It will make you a better mother."

NOTES

CHAPTER 3

MOM TRENDS

Start with a question. That's my advice to anyone who asks how I did it. Find me a group of successful mom entrepreneurs, and I bet the majority of them started a business because they were stumped. I believe the best companies start with the question:"…why doesn't this exist?"

Momtrends started with that premise. The question: "Why wasn't anyone publishing blog posts that I wanted to read, and that solved my problems!"

The short answer to why my business was started is: because I was annoyed. When I got impatient with the options available, I decided to solve my own problem. Fortunately, plenty of women have decided to join me for the ride!

In about seven years, I've been able to create a million-dollar brand out of my living room. Along the way, I took on zero debt and have been able to grow my business on my own schedule, at my own pace; a pace that worked for my family. I've been able to continually capitalize on growth opportunities as my daughters have grown. And never, ever have I had to ask for permission along the way.

Asking for permission to do things stinks.

Before having children, I spent nearly a decade working at Ralph Lauren in the stores of corporate offices. Looking around at the moms at Ralph Lauren, I couldn't locate a lot of role models.

I saw a lot of women making tremendous strides in career and contributing to an excellent corporation, but there were significant sacrifices made to family and relationships along the way. The feminist in me is glad that my "sisters" are climbing the ladder and securing positions in boardrooms, but I didn't want to have to ask anyone for permission to spend time with my family, or to travel and learn.

When it was time to start thinking about a family, I wanted to do it on my terms, not the corporate way. I don't mind "leaning in" if it's on projects that matter, and when I can do that leaning from a scenic spot.

Fortunately for me, I've been a good saver. My father told me early on to start socking away money in my 401K, and I made two great investments in apartments in my 20s. When I stepped off the corporate track in 2003, I had over $400,000 in savings.

I had zero debt, a great resume, a degree from Vanderbilt University, and more than anything else, the confidence in myself to take some risks.

Risk #1 was to quit my job with absolutely nothing lined up next. I spent all of 2004 traveling with my then boyfriend, now husband. We eloped on a trip in Bhutan (long story for another book, perhaps). In all, we traveled to 22 countries, living out of backpacks. When we returned to NYC, I'd been away from the city and out of work for a year. It was the perfect opportunity to reinvent myself.

I came back completely changed, and a horrible candidate for a corporate job - having a year of freedom to do what I wanted, when I wanted, changed me forever. I'd gotten a taste of freedom, and I wasn't looking back. Quickly making a traditional office even LESS appealing was the joyous news that I became pregnant.

Now I was expecting and looking for a career change. Many things interested me, travel, fashion, non-profit work, and writing - especially writing. My husband and I were living in an affordable area of Brooklyn, our expenses were minimal, and I still had plenty of savings. I had the luxury to continue taking risks.

I went to NYC's New School, and took a journalism course. Most of the kids in the class were taking the course for credit. I took it for fun. I didn't care that I was 10+ years older than all the other students. I was ready to learn. With a little encouragement from my professor, I submitted some pitches to local Brooklyn papers to cover events. I scored a job on my first try, and earned a whopping $50 freelance fee.

Even if the paycheck stunk, I was hooked. Getting paid to write rocked.

Soon, I was looking for more outlets that wanted to pay me to write. I wanted to work in my fashion background, but all my pitches to glossy magazines got repeatedly turned down. Were my ideas bad? I didn't think so. I just kept looking for outlets that wanted to hear my voice.

Slowly I built a respectable freelance business working for about a dozen different editors and magazine. As I gained experience, my confidence grew. Writing for other people turned out to be incredibly low-paying and frustrating. There were so many things I wanted to research and write about that I couldn't find a proper home for, and couldn't "sell" to an editor.

I wanted to write about stylish nurseries that suited my Ralph Lauren tastes, but fit my Brooklyn Food Co-Op budget. I wanted to wear my old $1,000 Manolo Blahniks from my Madison Avenue days with $25 cargo pants purchased from the Target across the street.

In 2007, I was seeing all these blogspot urls pop up. Women were using blogs to write deeply personal parenting essays. Why couldn't I use a blog to write about what I wanted to read - about living a stylish and fabulous life with less time, energy, and money! It's possible to have it all - you just needed to know where to look.

I've always been generous with my resources. If I found a great new restaurant, salon, or boutique, my instinct wouldn't be to hoard the resource; I wanted to share. My blog would be the ultimate sharing hub for my girlfriends.

As I was slowly finding my voice and audience on Momtrends. blogspot.com, I was also contributing a ton of articles to a large site called Babble.com. I pushed hundreds of strollers to road test the best rides. Often, the strollers I loved and the gear I blessed as the "best" was quite expensive. My Babble articles got some wrath in the comment feed.

"Who can afford a $250 diaper bag!", or "Who in her right mind needs a $1,000 stroller?" Increasingly, Momtrends became a spot where I found kindred spirits. Women who thought a $1,000 Bugaboo stroller didn't seem so crazy if it was your main means of transportation, and you lived in the city.

When I had my first daughter, I didn't own a car. My "wheels" were the NYC subway, Brooklyn buses, and my stroller. For me, it was pretty easy to justify spending $500 on a stroller (no, I never got the Bugaboo, but it was a great ride!). On Momtrends, no one pushed back on pricing. Our community was equally concerned about aesthetics and price.

Great entrepreneurs give themselves permission to fail. In 2009, I quit 75 percent of my freelance jobs and decided to dedicate myself to Momtrends. I wanted to see if I could grow it into a viable business. I didn't want my husband to fund any of it. I wanted the company to succeed or fail on my terms. That meant keeping things lean and benefiting from the budding boom of blogging.

The good news about my business was there was zero overhead. I worked from home around the girls' naps and sleep schedules.

In the first two years, traffic was growing slowly, but steadily. When we added Twitter to the equation in 2009, we saw a huge boost in traffic.

Many bloggers wear all the hats of their brand. They are Editor, Sales Manager, Event Director, and Office Manager. Even back in 2009, I was thinking bigger than that. I wanted a team; I couldn't pay much, but I could romance my vision.

Team Member One was found at a church toddler playgroup. Brooke and I met while our kids were gnawing on blocks. I'm not quite sure how I convinced her to team up with me on an unproven brand, but my passion must have been a selling point. We agreed that she would sell advertising from Momtrends on a commission structure. The more she sold, the more she made. We still have that arrangement today. Brooke has grown her representation into the company Power Moms Media, and she sells millions of dollars in marketing and research packages a year. All because someone asked her, "What if we try this?"

The first year we generated $7,500 in sales (mostly small banner ads). It was a start. I decided that I wanted to do some marketing to NYC moms. That's where Team Member Two comes in.

I convinced a dear friend and consummate hostess, Sherri, to help me get into the event business. I thought it would be a great way to connect with readers and market the brand. Plus, every time you gather women in real life (offline), you're bound to get more information than anticipated.

Our first event just about cleared $5 - barely enough for a Starbucks trip. My scrappy Event Manager was a genius at getting free space, but we were ALL OVER THE PLACE with messaging. We had some personal shopping, some snacks, and some toy testing. It was tremendously fun and unfocused.

Thankfully, adding Sherri to the mix meant adding a critic and voice of reason. With each event, we were finding our "voice." Our events got prettier and prettier. We decided to focus on hosting online influencers and to leave other companies' hosted events for the general NYC population.

After each event, the three of us - Editorial, Marketing and Events - would go to dinner to hash out what worked and what didn't. I was blessed to work with two friends who had a knack for self-improvement. None of us took criticism personally. We all wanted to grow, learn, get better, and produce a better product... and make more money.

Opportunities started pouring in. By 2010, I couldn't handle the workload. I added an Editor. This was the first employee who was not directly producing revenue. She was fielding pitches and helping me cover all the NYC events. As a professional trend spotter, I lived in the best city in the world. Every new product launch came through NYC. From 2009-2011, I attended every launch, product review, showcase, and press preview I could. I passed out cards and networked like mad. And it worked. Our tiny little brand was gaining readership and credibility. We let other blogs chase deals, coupons, and parenting trends. Momtrends focused on style-based editorial. We found our niche and we set out to do it better and better every year.

2012-2015 saw rapid growth. I carefully added team members when the work-load got out of hand. I was always extremely careful to hire only when the workload got to be overwhelming. I never wanted to "overhire" and have to be in the position of firing someone because our numbers didn't look good.

Solving problems was the key. Moms needed us. They needed to know what to wear, where to go on vacation, which stroller to buy, and how to mix a great cocktail (because date night is often a Friday night in). And we were there to help. Not as a know-it-all, but as a friend in-the-know. The girlfriend with the enviable contact list; the BFF who will give you an honest opinion when you are swimsuit shopping; and the bestie who is there to tell you there's no such thing a perfect mom. We're relentlessly positive, we strive to be pretty, we inspire women to try something new, and we believe in being social and sharing.

POSITIVE

Our Site is the girlfriend you always look forward to bumping into at yoga class. She makes you feel better about yourself and is always in the know. We don't bash women, moms, or the tough choices they make; we share best practices in the hope of making motherhood a lot more fashionable and fun.

INSPIRING

When it comes to the challenges of modern motherhood, our trend reporting delivers fresh ideas and innnovative solutions. Looking for a new experience or innovative way to solve a problem? You've come to the right place.

PRETTY

Appealing images, succinct writing and clean design are essential. Our readers are busy, savvy women; a visit to Momtrends is a mini vacation. All our features must meet our impeccable style standards.

SOCIAL

We put the social back into media, and love hearing about the trends that our readers find most compelling. This is a conversation; we welcome comments, criticism and tips from our community.

Once we had a mission statement (and every brand or business needs a mission statement), it was easy to decide what editorial fit on our pages and which brands were a match for us.

Good timing helps too. I've been lucky enough to witness the evolution in digital media spending. Each year we see more and more money being shifted from traditional media to online publications, and we're there to help and reap the rewards.

While we love helping brands spend money, we really love being able to help them solve problems. Client problems boil down to two things:

◊ They need to reach affluent, engaged moms who care about style.

◊ They need to find other bloggers who have strong networks.

I never tout myself as the smartest business woman, the best writer, or the most stylish dresser. What I do better than most, is hustle. Early on, clients were wowed by my professionalism, ability to meet deadlines, and follow-up.

At the end of a project, I kept hearing the same thing, "I wish there were more of you." This got me thinking that I, in fact, did "know more of me." ...Well not me exactly, but I had marvelous connections with blogging friends. Why couldn't I gather some peers to deliver great social media posts? A new segment of our business began. We called it Momtrends Blogger Outreach. We match bloggers up to campaigns for some of our favorite bands - like Hickory Farms, Hershey's, Chase Bank, Amwell Healthcare, and more. Bloggers love us for providing new financial opportunities, and brands adore us for delivering results.

Whenever I spot a hole in the marketplace, I jump in. It doesn't always work, but when I see inefficiencies, it makes me crazy. Seeing brands waste good money on bad events still makes me twitchy.

A recent Volvo test drive event in California is a case in point. I went out there as a brand fan, knowing in my bones that Volvo needs to be marketing to moms directly. They are wasting money on television and traditional media. I invested time and energy to woo the client. I haven't convinced them to spend a dime with me yet, but usually my persistence pays off, and my instincts are reliable.

I know which stories and brands will resonate with my readers. My dogged pursuit of the best brands for my blog has reaped great rewards.

What else works? Turning down business that doesn't make sense. It's hard to turn down a five-figure deal with a fast food chain after a few slow months, but we do it every time. I don't want a reader scratching her head when she sees me hawking fries after spending a decade encouraging readers to try to cook more homemade meals.

Authenticity and trust mean more than fast and furious growth.

I want this brand around for decades to come.

Now we're a team of 10. I'm proud and inspired by the women I work with. Each day they bring a level of awesome to everything we do. We've moved out of my home, and in to shared space in Brooklyn called We Work.

My team is an interesting mix. Nine out of ten of us have children (one employee has grandchildren - that's my mom). We range in age from 27-67, and we live in four different states. What we share is a common belief that motherhood can and should be fabulous. Each editorial meeting starts with asking: how we can delight our reader? What is she not getting right now, and what does she need more of? Analytics, social media feedback, and interaction at events fuel our research. We're never happy with what we did last year. Over the years, we've strived to build our community by bringing in new moms. A big part of that is storytelling through pictures. We're using original photographs and producing edited videos. The goal - drawing new moms in with images and keeping them engaged through storytelling and problem solving.

Do we do it perfectly every time?

Nope. But we never stop striving for better.

The same goes for parenting. Am I a perfect mom? Not even close. The dance between business and family is a tricky one where the tempo often changes.

Since starting my business almost a decade ago, I refuse to stop asking questions. It's served me well.

What problem are you ready to solve as a #MomBoss?

NOTES

Chapter 4

TOUGH LOVE

No one hands a Mom Boss opportunity on a silver platter and does all the hard work for her.

Mom Bosses invariably have a bumpy path to success. Along the way, they have to muster up an inner voice that gives them tough love. Mom bosses know the road is long and the challenges are big, but they also know they are capable, strong, and smart. There comes a point in the creation of every business where hard decisions have to be made. Money is often sacrificed, sleep is lost, and tears are wept.

Leaving the safety net of working for others is risky. There's no guarantee of income or benefits. I CAN guarantee you'll work long hours and that no successful Mom Boss has it easy 100 percent of the time. Before jumping into the world of self employment, you should ask yourself the hard questions:

Are you financially stable enough to make less?

Can you give up on the social atmosphere of your workplace?

Will you be productive while working in
an unstructured environment?

Do you have the wherewithal to be Head of IT, HR,
Marketing, Sales, Product Development and Janitorial?

Being a Mom Boss is no joke. Your work can be like wrangling a cranky toddler into a stroller - unwieldy and unpleasant. It can also be the most fulfilling work you'll ever do. But let's be clear, you've got to be passionate and purposeful to make it work. You've got to have a whole lot of tough love for yourself, because no one is going to do the hard work for you.

Is a Mom Boss born, or is she made? The answer is both. Some are thrust into greatness due to circumstances. Connie Peters, Founder and CEO of Modern Mama Media, didn't set out to become a digital media powerhouse. She remade her career when her workplace wouldn't budge on family time. Rather than continuing to get buried under her workload, she flexed her startup muscles and went to work - for herself. Other moms are more like GG Benitez. Prior to becoming a successful Mom Boss, she had several jobs where she tapped into her prodigious talents; she knew she had the drive and ambition to lead a business. It wasn't until after having three kids that she truly fulfilled her potential as the CEO of the thriving company, GG Benitez PR.

What both women have in common is smarts, skills, and the willingness to take a few risks. Let's start with Connie. Before starting Modern Mama, Connie was a software engineer in Vancouver. When her company nixed her plans to work part-time, she left. While it's maddening that many companies have zero flexibility for working parents, it was just the kick in the pants Connie needed to start her company.

Connie went back to work full time after having both of her older girls. The third child prompted her to want to scale back on work. When she returned to work after her maternity leave, she asked for reduced hours at a reduced salary, but was turned down. Connie quit four months after returning to work. Within a year of leaving a job that demanded "all or nothing" from her, she launched Modern Mama.

Modern Mama is an online hub for moms. Connie manages a network of sites that offer Canadian families the best in events and activities; it's all about getting moms out of the house and connected to other moms. Connie runs the business as a licensed model, overseeing City Managers in various cities throughout Canada. They purchase a license to operate under the Modern Mama Trademark, and use Connie's successful business model.

Now she works from home and, as she puts it, can take, "ownership of my own success." Most days, Connie works from her kitchen and oversees her kids' activities. On a typical day, she drops off the kids at school and then heads to "work" until 2pm. Work could be a lunch meeting or an online coaching call with a licensed mom writers. From two to five she runs the kids (now ages 12, 10, and 7) around to music lessons and other activities. Connie makes the most of her shuttling time. While the kids are in lessons she uses the time to engage with her community on social media. After pickup and snacks or activities, she jumps back on the computer for a couple of hours of work. Sometimes she works four hours a day, othertimes it's more like ten. She's got to manage her time well.

When I asked Connie to define her success, she said, "I'm able to be at home with my kids, work around their schedules, and be there for field trips and volunteer when I want to." And let's not forget the financial gains. After eight years, her business' revenue is exceeding her IT salary. While she doesn't take home that amount, she's investing in herself and reaping the emotional and financial rewards. Plus, now the harder she works, the greater the financial benefit she reaps. Does she have regrets? Not many. Connie says, "I think it would be entirely impossible for me to work in a traditional office now, reporting to someone else when I am so accustomed to being my own boss, and loving it."

Timing is everything for becoming a Mom Boss. Spotting an opportunity and taking the leap takes guts. Circumstances often thrust women into roles they never anticipated. Sometimes, Mom Bosses don't even have time to think about all the "what ifs" of being a leader.

GG Benitez says she was born to lead: "Whatever I've put my mind to, I've been able to achieve. I set a goal and get it done." Clearly, a strong work ethic was not a problem for GG, and she's got a habit of making her own luck.

Failure was not an option for GG when she graduated from college as a young, single mom. "I was broke, and need a job that paid well with room for advancement," GG says about her post-college job in pharmaceutical sales.

The young mom received accolades for her numbers, and earned big paychecks as a top salesperson in southern California. The financial rewards were important to GG, so that she could afford to live in a great school district for her daughter.

Eventually, GG left her sales career when she remarried and had two additional children. Working hard and meeting goals was never a problem for this California mom. The problem was finding a career where she could be independent.

For a while, she dabbled in real estate, jewelry sales, and ultimately launched a mommy and me clothing line called Tuni & G. The clothing line gained a huge celebrity mom following, and GG was able to land lots of press for the line - but it never took off financially. When the economy tanked in 2008, it was time for GG to get serious again. Dabbling wasn't going to help contribute to her family's bills. Through a bit of serendipity, a client appeared when GG got an order for her clothing line. Instead of just telling the caller that the line had been discontinued, GG asked questions, and more questions, and figured out that the caller needed a PR firm.

Thinking quickly, GG scored the opportunity to pitch the business. Within a week of the call, GG reinvented herself as a publicist. Eight years later, GG runs a successful boutique PR agency. She's an expert at getting products placed with celebrities, and has enviable connections in the entertainment industry.

How does she manage her growing brand? Carefully and imperfectly. GG admits that she overcompensated at first. As a startup CEO she threw herself into overdrive, being available 24/7 for her clients. With success under her belt, and long-term relationships with happy clients, she's been settling into a comfortable role as a Mom Boss. "It's tough for me to say I'm going to be traveling when a client calls me to ask for a meeting," GG says. "But my kids are only this age (her oldest just graduated from college; her younger two are 10 and 11) for so long, I want to enjoy them." She has a newfound respect for family time. She's still working with the same passion to promote her clients; she's just managing her time better.

Being a good Mom Boss means being self-critical, too. No one is going to tell you to shut the laptop and go to bed. GG willed herself to succeed, and admits to being "a workhorse." Now she has to will herself to put up the "out of office" message on her computer.

Balance isn't easy as a Mom Boss. We're all working to get it right. We've got to manage ourselves and our expectations, as well as the business. However, we never have to report to domineering bosses. For GG and Connie, and all the other Mob Bosses out there, success comes with sacrifice.

Time for a little more tough love; most Mom Bosses don't have someone hand them a business plan and $50,000 in startup capital. Before you launch into a business like Connie and GG, take these s for prepping to become a Mom Boss. First, start building a business nest egg. Stash away as much of your salary as you can to cover the hit to your income when you start your business. Figure out your benefit situation. You might be eligible for COBRA benefits, or if you're married or in a legally recognized relationship, you might be able to get you and your family on your partner's plan.

Don't be disillusioned. The money won't start rolling in right away. There are ways you can creatively lighten the load on your family budget as you enter into startup mode:

Cut down on childcare costs. Babysitting is expensive. In the beginning, try to pay for as little childcare as possible. Work around your children's nap/school/activity schedule.

Don't eat out. Start making your own coffee/lunch/breakfast. When I added up the expense of office rent, I knew I need to do two things. One, continue to increase sales; two, cut costs elsewhere. I used to work in cafes when the kids were home from school and I had projects. I got hooked on Starbuck's iced tea and Le Pain Quotidien salads. I was easily spending $60 a week on meals out of the house. That's $240 a month. That was half of my first month's rent at We Work in DUMBO. And THEY provide coffee and tea for free.

Take on freelance assignments in your field. When I started Momtrends, I was also working for other sites. My freelance income helped cover my expenses. I never had to dip into my savings to build my brand. Once sales increased at Momtrends, I let go of my freelance gigs.

It's not going to be easy to give up that delicious cup of Starbucks java, or your morning muffin - but this chapter is about tough love. Every dollar you save is worth two that you have to collect from clients. Budget smart, and then when the money starts coming in, the afternoon coffee runs will be so much sweeter. Discipline and tough love are essential for Mom Bosses.

Chapter 5

LIKE A BOSS - QUIZ

Now comes the fun part:

Matching your personality and skills to a #MomBoss career.

You know you want a lifestyle that is flexible and fulfilling, but did you know there are a vast array of options for you?

To make things easier, here's a #MomBoss quiz. As a girl, I went right to the quizzes in the glossy magazines I hoarded. A little introspection and analysis are just the things to break a girl out of a rut.

Channel your inner eighth grader, and take this quiz with brutal honesty. Don't answer what you think you should, let your heart be the guide. Just like Sister Margaret said in sixth grade to discourage looking at someone else's answers, "When you cheat, the only one you cheat is yourself."

1. Where do you prefer to work?

___ **A.** My kitchen table after the kids go to school, and the house is quiet.

___ **B.** A bustling café with loads of people around.

___ **C.** I can work anywhere, anytime as long as I'm inspired. Just give me wifi or a notebook.

2. I prefer to work:

___ **A.** Alone.

___ **B.** On a team.

___ **C.** With a small group I trust.

3. When it comes to earning money, my needs are:

___ **A.** Flexible. I'm ok with the ebb and flow of being self employed.

___ **B.** I like the independence money gives me. My earnings help fund family vacations, the kids extracurricular activities, and my blowout habit at DryBar.

___ **C.** Work isn't optional. I have to pay monthly bills, fund my kids' college account, **AND** save for my retirement.

4. I find inspiration:

___ **A.** From travel and reading.

___ **B.** From others.

___ **C.** Any time I encounter a problem without a good solution.

5. When it comes to dealing with rejection, I:

___ **A.** Prefer to do it via email, so I don't have to negotiate face to face.

___ **B.** Need a good friend to chat with.

___ **C.** Have thick skin, and really believe in myself.

6. I manage my time:

___ **A.** With a carefully organized day planner; family obligations are made in coded colors.

___ **B.** With a big whiteboard calendar in the kitchen. It's easy to erase and add and subtract things.

___ **C.** Digitally, and share my calendar with my partner. No detail goes unscheduled.

7. When plans change:

___ **A.** It takes me a while to adjust once I'm off my schedule. I'm a careful planner, and dislike when things don't go accordingly.

___ **B.** I roll with it. My car has snacks, blankets, chargers, and everything else to get me through a pivot in plans.

___ **C.** Grumble at first, and then grab my laptop and rearrange the schedule to prioritize what needs to get done.

8. When it comes to networking:

___ **A.** I prefer social media and having a filter as a safety net.

___ **B.** I'm a natural; strangers are just friends I haven't met yet.

___ **C.** I'm good in small groups, and connecting one-on-one.

9. Time to make a sales pitch. You:

___ **A.** Carefully plan and craft a PowerPoint presentation, and send a gorgeous, detailed file via email.

___ **B.** Aim to organize a coffee date where you can share your passion for business in person.

___ **C.** I start by crunching numbers and sales charts. I want to make a clear case for my Business, and I love telling the story of my brand.

10. What motivates you most?

___ **A.** Self satisfaction.

___ **B.** Acknowledgement from others.

___ **C.** Money and being visibly successful.

11. When you look five years into the future, your work will be:

___ **A.** Continuing to fuel my creative energy.

___ **B.** Have a team of 25.

___ **C.** Sold for $5 million dollars.

12. How do you deal with Mom Guilt?

___ **A.** Bake cookies and plan a special one hour LEGO festival to make up for a week that infringed on family time.

___ **B.** Rearrange my schedule and turn down new business to make family a priority.

___ **C.** Plan a family getawayafter your big sales period is behind you, and tell your family you'll all have unplugged time to look forward to in a few months.

Mostly As: *You're a Solo Artist.*

You don't need others around you to stay motivated. You take tremendous pride in your work and a job well done. You might be an introvert and get recharged by books and music. You prefer to communicate digitally, and like to work nontraditional hours around your family's schedule.

Careers to consider: Homebased consulting, Etsy shops, tutoring, writing, and art-centric businesses.

Mostly Bs: *You're a Team Mom.*

Chaos and last minute changes don't through you for a loop. You loved working at an office for the social access, but just can't make the structure work. Having people around fuels you, and you're a natural storyteller and salesperson.

Careers to consider: Real estate, interior design, homebased sales, travel agent/consultant, personal organizer.

Mostly Cs: *You're a Brand Builder.*

You've got a vision, and won't stop until you've reached your goals. While you may like working with people, it doesn't drive you. One thing is sure: you like being in charge, and aren't afraid to lead. You're goal oriented and willing to sacrifice short-term fun for long-term gains. You think big!

Careers to consider: Franchise owner, or startup maven. There's really only one option. Dream up your own business that doesn't exist, and go for it.

Though I hope you'll read all three chapters, the next three chapters are designed to hone in on the skills sets and personality traits identified in this quiz.

If your had answers that were all over the place (and that happens!), read all three chapters and take a look at the lives the women I interviewed have created.

Note: It's also ok to retake the quiz at different times in your life. Your answers in your 20s might not be the same as those in your 30s - it's ok to keep reinventing yourself. Frankly, it's a woman's prerogative to change her mind!

Chapter 6

SOLO ARTIST – PERSONALITY ONE

Solo Artist Moms are thrust into greatness. Few of them have mapped out career paths. While they may be ambitious about creating stunning works of art, they tend to not need a lot of external validation or suffer from narcissism.

Solo Artists tend to have specific, highly marketable skill sets. Such as graphic designers, photographers, artists, personal chefs, writers, lawyers, financial planners, etc. These women have extremely marketable skills. The savvy ones learn how to package their skills to others and do it on their own terms. Many of these Mom Bosses left traditional workplaces for of the same reasons the rest of us do: too many hours at an office where they were undervalued and treated like a commodity.

Freelance and contract work can be incredibly liberating. You take on as little or as much as you want - depending on your available time and your pursuit of income. From the dozens of women I talked with, money wasn't the big motivator. Mom Bosses know they have a finite amount of time with family. If cutting back on shopping, luxe vacations, and bigger homes means living a more passionate life, these women will gladly ditch the rat race for a work at home set-up.

Interestingly, the women who suffered corporate burnout weren't burnt out on performing skill, but instead on meetings, politics, and face time. When you cut that out of the work equation? It leaves a heck of a lot more time to spend with family and stay on top of your profession.

For the first few years of my career as a writer and entrepreneur, I was a Solo Artist. I seemed to be in an endless cycle of breastfeeding, cooking, diaper changing, and taking my tots to enrichment activities and playdates. Work was a life-line to my pre-kids self. But it was also very much in the back seat to my role as "mom."

I built up a tiny roster of digital publications I wrote for, and pecked away at my keyboard for 10-15 hours a week on projects and deadlines. I loved having work and building up a resume. It wasn't until I started Momtrends in 2007 though, that I felt like I was connecting the dots of my work experience and building something.

Kim-Marie Evans was in the same boat. Actually, her boat was much, much fuller. She has four kids. Yes, twice as many as I have, and she's built an enviable career as a Solo Artist.

Kim-Marie
@LuxuryTravelMom

@Momtrends I work at 4am when everyone is asleep. Then I still get to be mom and make cupcakes for class. I love having it all. Except sleep

The rawness of this tweet sums it up. Late nights are a reality, but the ownership of your time is an enormous upside. I suspect most Solo Artists are a little sleep deprived. It's a good thing this type of Mom Boss is energized by her work.

Kim Marie had a successful career in finance before she met her prince charming and started her family. Somewhere along the way to four kids, her career took a back seat. Her husband's financial success afforded her a life some might envy, but she felt something was missing.

Kim-Marie is now the Founder and Editor of TheLuxuryTravelMom. com a lifestyle site that focuses on jet-setting with kids in tow. Since her wanderlust and love of glamorous experiences didn't wane after the kids came along, she figured out a way to combine her love of travel and her desire to work. She started her business as a freelance contributor for print and online magazines. From there, she launched her own site meant to be a hub for all her travel writing. The site has become a thriving community, with highly engaged readers who love to travel. Now, her work is read by thousands of affluent moms who rely on Kim-Marie to tell them where to go and what to bring; she's become a trusted resource in the travel industry. She turned her lifeline into a career.

"I never knew how unhappy I would be being as 'just a mom.' I felt like I had lost all sense of myself and, along with that, my confidence. I went from working on a Wall Street trading floor, to feeling like I had to ask my husband for grocery money. Add on the lack of sleep and the mind numbing afternoons of Elmo and Friends, and I look back and wish I had gone back to work sooner," Kim-Marie says. The early days of motherhood look good in photos and on video, but reality is, they can be a slog. Mom Bosses gain self-worth and satisfaction that might not be as powerful as a toddler's hug and adoration, but it's a lot less sticky. The good news is there is space for sticky hugs AND cool paid projects in a Mom Boss' life.

Financial independence means a great deal to Mom Bosses. Some of them don't have a choice, they have to make money to support their families; others were raised as feminists, and don't feel right about not contributing to the family's economic situation; some gain a sense of worth seeing a check made out in their name with lots of zeros on the end.

Independence day for Kim-Marie came in the mail. "When I got my own Platinum card and started planning work trips without asking, I knew I was a Mom Boss."

Mom Bosses like Kim-Marie know that no one is going to hand them success. Solo Artists have to be especially motivated. Kim-Marie is an early bird: "I love to be up before the sun, I can get an entire day's worth of work done before breakfast. This means that I have time to make it to the school play and even cook dinner."

Solo Artist often need a little kick in the pants to get a business to thrive. Since Solo Artists are fired up by the work itself, many of them undervalue themselves. When it comes time to setting prices and pitching business, don't undervalue your time and talents. Learn to negotiate on your behalf, ask for more money and client referrals and keep track of your finances.

It's taken awhile, but Kim-Marie is becoming comfortable calling what she does a business and not having to make apologies for demanding better rates for her work. "I just became an LLC, so

I'm working through what that means for me tax-wise. Every year brings a new challenge financially; next, I want to add a retail arm to my site. There is no handbook for this type of work; I am constantly making it up as I go."

Leaving the office behind means saying goodbye to dreadfully long meetings that seemed to accomplish absolutely nothing. It means losing a community. Kim-Marie says, "The worst part of working for myself is when I wish I had another creative person to bounce ideas off of. I don't mind the billing, or even the drudge work of being a lone #momboss; there are just days I wish I had someone besides the dog to talk to." It's key for Solo Artists to build a community. It won't look like a traditional office, but it will serve as a virtual sounding board. Look to online groups and offline groups that can support your career efforts.

Don't leave your day job before taking a hard look at the work involved in becoming a successful Solo Artist. "No one sees that I'm up at 4:00 a.m. every day doing this. That my trips are not vacations, they are research trips," Kim-Marie says. However, becoming a highly respected travel writer and digital influencer was worth all the missed sleep for Kim-Marie.

Being a Solo Artist is also an opportunistic way to test the waters of a different career path. By day, Laura Venos is a career counselor at Georgetown University. But she's got a super power. At night, she goes to work attempting to undo the princessification of our girls. Laura's passion is putting a twist on classic fairies, with her self-published series of children's books called *The Royal Series*.

Solo Artists like Laura are driven by the creative process. It's not easy. After working eight to ten hours and spending time with family, she sets to work on her books. She says, "I have a strong urge to be creative, and it's hard to be creative in a traditional work environment." So she writes at night and makes it happen.

Working around motherhood and her day job, Laura finds time to build her brand up because she's looking for new ways to encourage girls to lead. Laura's got two young children and a job.

She didn't need to find something to fill her days; it was her passion that drove her to becoming a Mom Boss.

Here's something I hear from newly minted Mom Bosses again and again: "For me, it's less about how much money I make, and more about whether the time I'm putting into work is directly creating satisfaction in my life.

TAKING A PAY CUT TO GET A LIFE YOU LOVE SEEMS LIKE A FAIR TRADE.

Laura is excited and nervous about following her dreams. Launching new books and gaining young readers is thrilling, but "the worst part is the uncertainty and risk of whether the business will be successful enough to sustain." Solo Artists don't have a team to help dream up new products or business leads. Laura has to set the pace of her business, and she alone is responsible for the success or failure.

Many of the prominent bloggers that have found success from digital media seem gob smacked that they have turned a passion for writing and creating into a paying gig. Some of my favorite digital publishers were busy with just being a mom when blogs popped up. They turned a passion for food, writing, crafting, and photography into a business. There wasn't a road map or a business plan. They just made it up as they went along, fitting in recipe testing and writing between school drop-off and laundry. Now, many of these Solo Artists are earning six figures and have had to find help to support their creative endeavors.

For digital media stars like Hayley Morgan (TheTinyTwig.com), being a Solo Artist is the best. "I like that I can pivot quickly, and make decisions on the spot without having to consult with a ton of different people. Plus, [my business] can grow as I grow."

Flexibility, creativity, and passion. These are the cornerstones of life as a Solo Artist.

How to spot her: She prefers to work alone, but welcomes collaboration on projects. She tends to be introverted, and loves to read and dig into materials that fuel her work. She's detail oriented, and can manage a massive to-do list. Her work environment tends to be warm and nurturing, though you might spot her at a cafe with her notebook out. She can tune out the world when she's on deadline. The Solo Artist is a woman who is fueled by the work process and the end product, and takes tremendous pride in her creations.

Career options: Tutor, researcher, freelance writer, photographer, artist, personal chef, therapist, home-based consulting, Etsy shop owner, or art-centric business.

Reasons to love this life: The Solo Artist can create an extremely flexible work schedule. Solo Artists can take entire months off at a time; they can also arrange to work 10 days straight.

Pitfalls: As a lone wolf, the Solo Artist is always hustling for the next gig or contract. The financial hustle can be draining. And even the most introverted mom needs some good girl-chat now and then. Make sure to network with your peers and plan coffee dates with client to avoid isolation and develop your client base.

Chapter 7

BRAND BUILDER - PERSONALITY TWO

How are brands born? When it comes to Mom Boss brands, there's usually a hole in the marketplace just waiting to be filled.

Many Brand Builders start with an idea, and it takes hold of them; gnaws at them. It's the rare case that a Brand Builder says, "I just want to make loads of money," and then backs into a great idea and builds a fantastic team. I'm not going to say it never happens, but it's rare. What does happen, is that a mom feels passionate about a missing product or service and **CAN'T LET IT GO.**

I started Momtrends because I couldn't find a site like it on the internet. First, it filled my need. Fortunately, it turned out there were moms just like me out there, and brands that wanted to market to us.

When Momtrends hosted Jessica Alba for her NYC launch party for Honest back in 2009, I heard her story. She didn't want to use mysterious products on her kids. She started educating herself about ingredients in baby care products and the environmental impact of diapers. The young actress couldn't believe no one was making something better. That's how Honest Co. was born. Jessica morphed from actress to CEO because she couldn't find the right products for her kids. She was solving a problem.

Now I realize that not everyone has a billion-dollar idea. And that's ok. Small can be beautiful. Every day, my inbox is flooded with brand launches and Kickstarter requests for moms that are thinking big by starting small.

Many Brand Builders start as Solo Artist. Over the past decade of my career as a Mom Boss, I've morphed from a freelancer to a CEO. That's one of the great parts of being your own boss, your career can bend and flex as your kids hit different life stages.

AS YOUR AMBITION FIRES UP, YOU CAN EXPAND YOUR COMPANY.

The glory of building a brand is that it is intensely personal. The Mom Boss in charge can control the culture, quality, and speed of growth.

Brand Builders are idea generators. Corporate life with its rules and political landmines frustrated these women, and led them to seek something better.

With the risk of starting something new came great rewards for some Mom Bosses. It's intensely gratifying to get to call the shots and build a company where all the traditional rules go out the window. It's also tougher than the other two types of Mom Boss businesses. Women are 37 percent more likely than men to be self-funded. This means that not only do we come up with the big ideas, we also have to find the money to make our dreams a reality.

Brand Builders are more comfortable with risk than other types of Mom Bosses. Most brands requi re a bit of startup capital - even if it's just enough to buy a url and logo design. You'll either need content or inventory to launch a brand. This is going to require an investment of time, money, or both.

Then there's the human capital. If you need a sales team, you've got to slog through the requirements of getting your payroll set up with workmans' compensation, and unemployment taxes. If I could get the hours of my life spent surfing through the NY state bureaucracy to legally hire employees, I would be thrilled. Brand Builders need to be intensely driven and passionate, otherwise all these obstacles will be a drain on the energy of the business.

I worked as a freelance writer to cover the startup costs of Mom-trends. I didn't want to put expenses on my credit card and incur debt to launch my business. I also decided early on that the busi-ness was going to be content based, not commerce driven. I knew the huge outlays of cash needed to fund a product launch weren't for me. I was lucky that my passions were matched to a business with a relatively low barrier to entry. On the downside, there was a lot of competition; it's relatively easy to launch a new website catering to moms.

Brand Builders are able to look to the horizon and see beyond the mundane money issues and focus on vision of the future. They have to live a reality of a balanced budget, but never lose the drive to move forward. Uli Belenky is certainly never one to dwell on the past. She's a visionary designer who has created a beloved children's brand called Zutano.

Zutano was one of my early "discoveries" as a lifestyle blogger. As a young mom, I was drawn to bold colors and whimsical prints in baby boutiques. It was easy to love the clothes from this iconic brand. They combined comfort, quality, and playfulness. Dressing my girls in Zutano's leggings and dresses was a joy. As my career progressed, I got to meet the Vermont-based founders of Zutano, Michael and Uli Belenky. In addition to her two daughters, Ulit will tell you Zutano is her third child. Her personal stamp is on everything from the prints she develops, to the bucolic setting of her home office, to her extremely liberal new parent policy.

Born in Germany, Uli came to the US as an art director. When she found out she was expecting, she and Michael surveyed the children's clothing landscape and were dismayed. Everything they saw in stores was pink and blue. They wanted more creative clothes for their yet to be born child; so they launched Zutano.

The brand and the new baby arrived at almost the same time. The new parents threw themselves into parenting and the launch of the company. They started in New York, but relocated to rural Vermont to grow the brand and the family. Uli loved the freedom she was granted by being a boss - she could operate and grown her brand at her own speed. When you take the pressures of venture capitalist investments and meeting quarterly numbers out of the equation, it's easier to focus on design, quality, and building customer loyalty.

"When we first moved up to Vermont, it was a conscious decision to move a step slower. If we lived in NY, we would have had to grown the brand faster than we were ready for," Uli says. With NY rents and the pricey cost of labor, they would likely have had to bring on investors or degrade the quality of the fabrics to increase margins.

In Vermont, there weren't so many compromises to be made. They worked from home while an old barn was being restored to be the home office of Zutano. Everything moved at a pace the family could maintain. "Our kids were our focus, we wanted to have a really good balance."

Running the brand from Vermont meant Uli and Michael didn't have all the distractions of the NY fashion world. "For us, we focus on our core beliefs, not trends," Uli says. Uli steers where the collection will go each season. Her vision brings the brand to life.

The teams that Brand Builders gather benefit from the priorities of a Mom Boss. Zutano has a working parent policy that makes most women envious. It all started with Uli's babies. "They were always in the office, we always had our kids around," Uli says.

When one of their employees became pregnant, the Zutano maternity leave policy evolved. "The first employee to have a child while working at Zutano was our production manager. She had a very important role in the company. We said we would make it work for her to bring her baby to work. It worked for our kids, and we'll make it work for you," Uli says. Brand Builders know that protecting talent means being creative.

Uli created a **"maternity office"** with a crib, art work, toys, and changing station. It's a private room where a mom can breastfeed and enjoy time with their baby. "We came up with a system that works for us; the parent is the daycare provider," Uli says. In this set-up, the parent can be with the baby every day, and the baby's needs come first.

Zutano has had almost 25 babies come through their office over the years. Uil's proud of this job perk: "It's one of the most valuable benefits we've had." Plus, she boasts that it's wonderful to have that pint-sized inspiration around - baby models are just a few steps away. This policy helped Zutano stay authentic to who they are. Instead of seeing a problem ("oh no, we're losing an employee!"), Uli thought like a Brand Builder and came up with a solution.

Even if there are days the work/life balance goes off the rails (and there will be many, many of those), having a brand take off can be its own reward. For Uli, her two young girls saw a woman at the helm of a business. "Having a mother who was the leader of this business was a powerful influence and inspiration," Michael says. Both girls are grown now and have careers in the arts.

Brand Builders frequently attest that work and life blur together. And that can be a very good thing. When work feels like play, it's much harder to get burnt out. Uli says, "Private life and work life, it's all one thing."

According to *Bloomberg*, eight out of ten entrepreneurs who start businesses fail within the first 18 months. Mom Bosses need a really good idea to succeed. Nicole Smith has one, and it's called Flytographer.

Nicole lives in Victoria, Canada, and before she became a Mom Boss she spent time as a Microsoft Marketing Manager and Consultant. Her big idea happened while she was traveling. While in Paris on a girls' weekend, she hired a local friend to take candid photographs of her and her pal as they enjoyed the city together. Upon returning home with beautiful images that truly captured the spirit of her trip, Nicole had her epiphany: there needed to be a service that provided high-end vacation photography.

Launched in 2013, Flytographer is an online service which captures travel memories by connecting travelers with highly skilled, local photographers in cities around the world. Nicole mapped out a solid exit strategy. She continued to work full-time at Microsoft while she launched and ran Flytographer on weekends and at nights. The kids were the ones who helped convince her to take the big leap and leave the security of Microsoft. "My boys were five and seven, and I was burning out - I knew something had to give. I saw the business growing rapidly, customers were truly loving it, and I knew I had to take a bold risk," Nicole says.

In just two years, Nicole has grown the Flytographer network to 350 photographers in 175 destinations. She's landed investment funding to fuel her growth, and forged significant partnerships with global travel brands.

As Founder, Nicole does it all; she is in charge of growth and quality control. Nicole is hooked on the "creative freedom of building something."

Nicole's taste has defined the brand. She is discerning about all her photographers, and has put her aesthetic stamp on the offices, too. "Our office is very feminine, and full of beautiful customer photos from around the globe. It's fresh, modern, and full of natural light," Nicole says. A Brand Builder knows that the brand is more than the product they produce; it's also the office environment and culture.

Freedom has been key to Nicole's desire to continue to build Flytographer. "Success to me is having choices on how I spend my time. When you get to the point where you can chose to only do meaningful work you are truly passionate about, that is success," Nicole . Like all the Mom Bosses I met, Nicole's priorities shifted when her kids came along.

No one knows how much work is involved in a startup like a Mom Boss. Building a brand can be all-consuming. "It's like having a third child. And in the early days, it's like having a newborn. You are up late at night, get less sleep, don't understand why things aren't working, and get crap tossed at you unexpectedly," Nicole says. But just like with children, the rewards can be awesome. Warning. Nicole says it best: "If you don't love your startup passionately - don't bother!"

As you're building a brand, sometimes you'll have a day of one parenting fail after the next. Just keep moving towards your goals; sometimes you hit it big.

Julie Cole was one of the Founding moms behind Mabel's Labels (a brand which was recently sold for $12 million to Avery Labels), and a mom to six. She laughs at the notion of being a perfect mom and running a brand. Here's her advice: "Don't care about the state of your house. Don't obsess over what people think. Don't beat yourself up if the kids have hot dogs for dinner twice in a row. All these things don't matter. Leave guilt at the door. It's a waste of time. What matters is that you forge ahead, get down to work, and live your passion. It will make you a better mother."

One of Julie's big tips for Brand Building moms is to let go of the idea of perfection - but it's not easy. Julie lumps herself in with the rest of us as a "control freak." Brand Builders believe every detail reflect on the brand. Julie knows that to truly empower a team, you've got to let go.

It's also a testament to her belief in her brand that after the big pay day, Julie has stayed on. Now that she's passed off some of the management duties, she's focusing on relationship building and making sure Mabel's stays true to its core mission of helping moms. Julie's new role is to be the face of the brand. "At Mabel's Labels, we place a lot of value on relationships, and believe that great businesses are built on great relationships. As such, I blog, speak at moms groups, am active on social media – I do anything I can to connect with our market of moms." This is what Julie does all day. Many new companies overlook this - you may have the most clever invention, but if you're not connecting with your consumer, you're in trouble. Julie knows connection is essential. She lives and breathes her brand with every lunch she packs and every batch of laundry she folds.

Julie knows all about keeping kids' gear organized - that's why she's such an authentic leader. Her personality shines through on interviews and on social media. She embraces her imperfections, and celebrates her successes with equal enthusiasm. That's why other moms love her. She's the one who has a hug ready on a bad day, and a tip to make the next day go better.

As one of the more seasoned Brand Builders I spoke with, I also asked Julie about imitators. With success, they will pop up; you need a plan on how to recognize them. "Countless companies have popped up since we first started Mabel's Labels. We've remained the market leader because of our product innovation, and through our commitment to having a strong online community of moms," Julie says.

At the end of it all, after the numbers are crunched and checks are cashed, Brand Builders remain most proud of being able to build a brand and stay connected to family. For Julie, the blossoming of her business made her a better mom. According to Julie, her greatest accomplishment is helping her autistic son flourish. "I started Mabel's Labels partly as a result of my oldest child getting diagnosed with autism when he was three. He is now 16. He does well at school, has a lot of friends, plays hockey, has a black belt in taekwondo, works as a mentor for young kids with autism... and the list goes on and on."

Successful Brand Builders are the ones who can pivot quickly, learn from mistakes, and never stop listening to feedback. Brand Builders can be inventors, but most of the best Brand Builders also bring in savvy marketing skills, and a passion for solving problems. A desire to be better than yesterday propels them forward, and allows them to lead.

How to spot her: She's usually on her phone, and on the go. She's a connector of people, and constantly updates her contact list to see how she can help her friends solve problems. Her kids might not be perfectly dressed, but they are seeing a woman in power living her dream - and that's better than perfectly coiffed kids.

Career options: Launching new clothing lines, developing mom-friendly household products, building blog empires, creating family-friendly tech startups, or developing services that solve problems for other women.

Reasons to love this life: The sky is the limit. Dream big, work hard, and you might have the next Honest Company on your hands.

Pitfalls: It's lonely being boss. All the mistakes are yours. Running out of working capital before your product hits it big is devastating. Male entrepreneurs are 86 percent more likely to be VC funded than their female counterparts, and men are 59 percent more likely to secure angel investment.*

Chapter 8

TEAM MOM –
PERSONALITY THREE

Imagine making money while hanging out with your best friends and getting to play with things you love... like clothes, accessories, or beauty products. For Team Moms, this is a way of life - and for many of them, a way to earn six-figure incomes.

Unlike being a Brand Builder or Solo Artist, a Team Mom can build a career without having to invent something new. Much like buying into a franchise, Team Moms buy into businesses that have structure and a track record.

There are far fewer unknowns in the world of a Team Mom. Before you sign on however, let's backtrack a bit and talk about the history of this type of business.

You might hear the terms: social selling, multilevel marketing, network marketing, or direct selling. There's no store. The sales are done in homes and at social settings. Salespeople earn commissions not only for their own sales, but also for sales made by the people they recruit. In 2011, roughly 15.6 million Americans worked as salespeople for multi level marketing companies, according to the Direct Selling Association. Many of them are Team Moms.

One of the earliest examples of this type of business is Avon. In 1886, David H. McConnell decided to start an all-female, home-based salesforce to sell his cosmetics. The work was flexible and fun for these stay-at-home moms, and the sales were huge. McConnell figured out the secret sauce to selling - the influence of friendship. Studies show that women are highly influenced by peers. In fact, in a recent survey from Inc., 63 percent of all mothers said that they consider other moms the most credible experts when they have questions before purchasing a product.

Here's how it happens. A friend from your church invites you to a get-together - let's call her Ashley. You've always admired how put-together Ashley is, but you don't know her very well. Ashley has invited you to an at-home party for a brand she sells called JewelsSeasons (this is a fictitious brand, and I don't really know an Ashley). Ashley tells you she's been wearing JewelsSeasons this spring, and loves how they enhance the clothes she already owns. She can't wait to have you over to show you the new line.

You say sure, slightly out of guilt, slightly out of interest. If Ashley's a strong seller and the product is good, you're going to have a great time. You'll sip some wine, nibble on some salmon canapés, and shop. You touch the product and think, "hmmm, this jewelry is lovely!" You end up buying a few things, and eagerly sign on to host the next party at your home.

From there, things get interesting. Ashley helps you plan and execute the party. Your friends buy a ton of accessories. You start seeing the power of your network. At this party, you'll earn credits towards more purchases, or maybe even cash.

From there, you'll meet one-on-one with Ashley to talk about career opportunities. It's her job to build her sales force and increase her territory and commissions. She'll try to convince you to be part of her team. You like Ashley, you like the product, and you're ready to sign on.

The pitch is enticing. When things are working, the Team Mom money can be fantastic, and the work a true joy.

Wait.

You've got a choice to make, and some research to do. BestCompany.com lists more than 130 multi-level companies, and there are many that aren't listed there. Just as the Solo Artist and the Brand Builder need to research their niches, so does the Team Mom.

Then again, timing is everything; getting into a brand early matters. For Holly Rust, a Team Mom based in Chicago, the decision to join the Rodan + Fields skincare salesforce was instant. "I jumped right in after a ten minute phone conversation with an old coworker/ friend I respected. I knew in my gut that R+F was going to be huge, and my fear of missing out took over. I had not even tried the products yet. I knew these doctors created the billion dollar Proactiv brand, and that was enough for me," Rust says.

It's easy to get swept into things when you're given a smooth sales pitch - but things worked out well for Holly. She is now a successful team member of the Rodan + Fields skincare brand. Rodan + Fields has more than 12,000 associates selling anti-aging products in North America.

Holly was successful because she did a few smart things. First, she picked a winner. Some of that is luck, some is research. Second, she built a strong team and picked her team members wisely. Third, she had experience running a business.

Holly spent 12 years in corporate America in sales/marketing. In 2013, Holly left to focus on a writing career and to be a "more present mom." Holly focused exclusively on her writing career at first, and then built her Rodan + Fields business. As a Mom Boss, Holly knows how to leverage her past experiences to make herself a successful Team Mom career.

Currently, Holly has 112 people on her Rodan + Fields team. That means that every time a member of her team sells a $193 Redefine Regimen, Holly gets a cut. Since team building is a big part of success, Holly made it her mission to recruit excellence and support those beneath her. In her corporate life, Holly worked at a luxury hotel brand. She knew all about customer service. Her international team (made up of members spaning across the U.S. and Canada, and soon to be Australia) benefits from her pre-mom training.

Picking the right brand for you is essential. Holly says, "I personally love the brand and company, so selling for them is easy - but the number one driving force behind my motivation is my kids. I don't want them to have to do without, but I don't want to sacrifice all my time with them to make the income we need." Sounds familiar. Like the Brand Builder and Solo Artist, Holly figured out a way to utilize skills from her former corporate career to create a fulfilling life as a Mom Boss. Ask yourself:

WHAT SKILL CAN YOU TAP INTO TO CREATE YOUR PERFECT MOM BOSS CAREER?

Freedom of time is a big deal for Holly and most Team Moms. In general, multi-level marketing careers offer very flexible hours. Team Moms can also work from just about anywhere - no office is needed. Holly says the schedule was a huge draw for her, "I love to be able to be there for my boys. I missed so much of my older son's life when I was in corporate life, and I still carry guilt to this day."

Holly's children are now five and two, and this path has allowed her to be present for her kids and get involved in her community. "I wouldn't get the chance to volunteer at my children's preschool if I didn't have flexibility," Holly says.

The hustle to get business going will be big at the beginning, but once it's up and running, the upsides are huge. Imagine running your calendar instead of being run by it. Freedom of time is a major tool Holly uses to motivate her downline. "Family always comes first, and our corporate team continuously promotes this. If you qualify for an incentive trip, then they will work around your family's schedule. They also encourage you to bring your baby to meetings and conventions; then you're able to nurse and not have to leave your baby behind," Holly says.

Team Moms have some compelling success stories. As Holly tells it, after only a few years she is able to work about 5-10 hours a week on average - and she is set to make more than $100,000 this year. That's the magic of multi-level marketing; time it right, build a good team, and you're golden.

Not every multi-level marketing business ends with this happily ever after tale. It's savvy to look for a brand that has a track record of success. Sadly, not all opportunities are created equally. The shady direct sales companies are called pyramid schemes, and they lure in victims with the promise of fancy cars, ritzy vacations and, of course, heaps of cash.

You've got to do your research.

According to the FTC, not all multilevel marketing plans are legitimate. Here's the key: if the money you make is based on the number of people you recruit and your sales to them, the FTC says the business is not legitimate. It's a pyramid scheme. Pyramid schemes are illegal, and you are very likely to lose money investing in them. Make sure there is something legitimate to sell.

Holly Hanna has earned a reputation as a watchdog for moms who work at home. She's the Founder and CEO of The Work at Home Woman. She is an advocate for telecommuting and home-based businesses that empower women to balance life on their own terms, and has vetted numerous direct sales companies. She offers this advice in her ebook:

"When choosing a home party business opportunity, you'll want to make sure that you're doing business with a reputable company. Look for companies that have an affiliation with the Direct Selling Association (DSA), which promotes ethical business practices in the direct sales market. Check out the Better Business Bureau (BBB) website, make sure that they have an excellent rating and all customer grievances have been resolved. Also, look around on Google and see if there are any negative reviews or complaints.

"One of the best ways to learn about a company is to talk to current and past consultants. Find out what they like and don't like about the company. See if you can find out what the retention rate is, and if consultants are paid on time. By putting in some additional effort on the front end, you can potentially divert an unpleasant experience on the backend."

For more of Holly's tips visit

http://www.theworkathomewoman.com/

Here's the upside: $30 billion in sales are generated each year by multi-level marketing, with commission rates ranging from 10-60 percent - that's some big money funneled into the Mom Boss economy.

Find out how much your initial investment will be. The "buy in" is different with each organization, but there are usually start up costs. Here's the good news: for the legitimate brands, the initial investment is nothing like the costs of opening an office or a boutique. Plus, you have a built-in marketing machine - the parent brand is helping you along the way.

Once you decide on this path, it's time to hone your pitch. Multi-level marketing or direct sales is part marketing, and part sales. The Team Mom is compensated not only for the sales she generates, but also for the sales of the other salespeople she's recruited. This recruited salesforce is referred to as the participant's "downline" - the downline can help you reap big rewards. Remember Ashley? If you join her team she'll get to keep a percentage of every sale you make in addition to her own sales. You are part of her downline. There's a big incentive there for her to grow her team. This is where the money gets interesting. This is why it's called "multi-level marketing."

But it's not all about the money. Team Moms also thrive on the social elements. Moms are drawn to this type of business because it can be social and interactive, but quite independent as well.

Kate Stines is a very successful member of the Stella & Dot sales team. For the past six years, this South Carolina mom has been making sure her friends and family are well outfitted in this colorful brand of jewelry and accessories.

At the first event she hosted, Kate earned $900. She thought "... well that was FUN!!"The mom of three doesn't just find the money enthralling, she loves using her degree in Retail Fashion Merchandising while being able to homeschool her kids. Plus, Kate just loves that when she is working she is "not a wife, not just a mom... I'm just me!"

Kate's infectiously positive attitude has led her to build a team of more than 50 Stella & Dot representatives. Most direct selling companies require (or highly suggest) members attend one or two training sessions a year. For Kate, this bit of travel is a highlight. Stella & Dot calls the yearly event the Hoopla. There, they not only preview new collections, but also celebrate sales performance of individuals and teams.

Team Moms know how to make work feel like play. "When you have a passion for the product and a love for sharing it, selling just fits into your life," Kate says.

For many, the biggest hurdle is getting over the thought of being a salesperson. There is an argument as to whether great salespeople are made or born; I think both. You've got to be outgoing, but you can also train an outgoing woman into becoming a super seller Team Mom. Knowledge breeds confidence.

Holly Rust says, "I definitely think anyone can learn how to sell, especially in network marketing. Network marketing is all about sharing and relationship building - which women do very well. I do think, however, that some women are natural born leaders."

Of course, we've all heard stories of friends who started and ended these businesses. The key with running a successful direct sales business is to first and foremost believe in the product. Then, perform due diligence on the company to make sure you are set up for success.

It's all about finding a sales opportunity that works for your life. Don't worry if you don't think you can sell! If you're good at making friends, keeping in touch, and staying organized, this could be your calling.

Just Part cheerleader, part energizer bunny, a Team Mom is tireless. She's a connector of people and loves sharing her finds with others.

How to spot her: She's surrounded by people and usually laughing. She's constantly sharing articles and recipes on social media, and celebrating the successes of her friends. She is likely to be very involved in church or PTA, and a frequent volunteer.

Career options: Direct Sales (aka multi-level marketing) of essential oils, fashion, health and beauty products, kitchen gear, and much, much more.

Reasons to love this life: Extremely flexible hours, low startup costs, and a very social work life.

Pitfalls: You've got to learn to love selling.

Chapter 9

SETTING UP SHOP

You've decided on your business model; now you need to set up shop. Thanks to technology, there have never been more opportunities for mom entrepreneurs. The good news is, becoming a Mom Boss has never been easier.

Getting going is really a four-step process. Don't worry if you've already started with a few of these action items. While this is the IDEAL order, many women back into their businesses as I did. They start creating, networking, and selling before they figure out they've got a viable business.

Four Steps to #SettingUpShop:

◊ **Map Out a Business Plan**

◊ **Meet with Advisors**

◊ **Create Your Brand**

◊ **Set Up Your Interface**

These four steps can take years, or weeks; it depends on how ambitious you are, and how much money you need to get going. As a naive blogger, I started executing without a plan or strong branding. It would've made life easier to go through the natural progression, but know this - follow your instincts and fit in the four steps where you can.

Don't think you've got to go get an MBA to map out your plan. You need a basic framework that shows how much you need to put into the business to get started, and how you anticipate getting revenue. In addition to figuring out how you are going to make money, you need to anticipate the timing of your launch.

At the very least you need to know:

◊ **One year of anticipated sales**

◊ **One year of anticipated expenses
(we'll go more into this in Chapter 10)**

◊ **Without projecting these two things, you'll never know if you have a hobby or a business.**

The next part of your plan involves timing. If you're reading this book, you've either got kids or will soon have them. Would I advise becoming a #MomBoss in your third trimester? Probably not. Likewise, if you are currently in a job, you need to time your exit strategy. When can you financially leave your job behind? It's nice to have a little economic cushion before you leap into your #MomBoss phase.

A plan needs to answer these questions:

◊ **How much time can I devote to this business?**

◊ **How much startup cash am I going to need for this business?**

◊ **Do I need additional training skills? How am I going to get them?**

◊ **What are my goals? (These should be both financial and personal.)**

Mom Boss Tip

Write down these goals and print them. Check-in every few months to make sure you are on track.

_____

_____

_____

_____

If you need to take out a loan, you'll need to develop a much more detailed plan - but even if you just plan to use your own blood, sweat, and tears, you should know what the end goal is, and the steps you have to take to get there. Of course, things are going to change along the way. There will be curve balls; like any good recipe, you need the basic ingredients to get going.

For Kate Whyte, a LCSW (licensed clinical social worker), careful planning allowed her to leave her legal career and pursue her passion to help others. For more than a decade, Kate was a lawyer. She practiced litigation for a large Wall Street law firm, earned a large salary, and had outward success. Now, Kate is both a psychotherapist and a psychoanalysis specializing in infertility and adoption.

Kate started mapping out the #MomBoss chapter of her career while she was General Counsel for a large tech company. Kate was ready to start a family, and knew something had to change. "I worked all the time, and traveled a lot," Kate says. While she enjoyed her work as a lawyer, and made excellent money, she wanted a more flexible schedule. Kate knew her current job wasn't a fit for the type of mom she aimed to be.

She needed a plan. "Everyone says do what you love. I always loved psychology and I felt that I would love to be a therapist," Kate says. Before she made the leap, she did research. "I had spent a great deal of time and money to become a lawyer, and I enjoyed many aspects of that job." Kate took steps to create the change she craved. It's not an accident that she rose through the ranks of her legal career. Here drive and talent took her far. It was time to see where else her skills could take her.

Kate figured out how to leverage her past to create her best future. Working with a therapist, Kate mapped out a transition plan. "I found many of my previous skills and strengths as a lawyer translated to therapy as a profession," Kate says. She's analytical, comfortable with counseling, and enjoys interacting with people.

She went to school to get her LCSW, and completed the degree in 16 months. In less than two years, Kate started earning income in her chosen field. Now Kate is in a private practice in the West Village of NYC. To save on overhead, she shares office space. She rents from another therapist - a savvy move since she only pays for the office when she uses it, and doesn't have to rent or buy office furniture.

It's not all perfection though. Kate does have to wrestle lots of paperwork in her role. She no longer has a support staff like she did in her legal career. She'll happily trade a little small business bureaucracy for time with her family, though.

"TO ME, SUCCESS IS DEFINED AS HAVING THE TIME AND MONEY TO LIVE A LIFE DOING WHAT YOU LOVE," KATE SAYS.

Kate's equation is a solid one: hard work plus a solid plan, and you've got a good recipe for Mom Boss success.

Seek and ye shall find. Once you know what you want to do, hunt down a mentor or advisor to make the process easier. Kate took the time to seek out an advisor currently working in the field. Seeking guidance from peers in your chosen career can save you a lot of anguish. Tap your network of friends and family to find women and men who can help. Ask the tough questions, and do your homework. For me, taking a class in journalism was a great step towards my ultimate success. My professor was a valuable resource. It's not just being told what works, it's also figuring out what doesn't. I quickly decided that living for the next scoop wasn't for me. I didn't want to be a journalist.

Mom Boss Tip

Don't be afraid to find out what you DON'T want to do.

Find business owners who have succeeded and failed. If you are thinking about joining a direct sales team, find someone that has dropped out of this work and ask her why. Don't just look for the success stories.

YOU CAN LEARN JUST AS MUCH FROM FAILURE AS SUCCESS.

Once you've settled in on the work life you want to create and have a model that you think will make money, it's time to brand. Your brand is a story. It communicates with customers what they can expect from you. Your brand is more than your name and logo; it's how you plan to do business. All the work you did to decide on the business has led you to this point. Now you have to figure out how to communicate your vision to your clients.

Raquel Langworthy has made a career out of helping Mom Bosses turn a business into a brand. As the Founder of Untamed Studios, Raquel is both a Mom Boss and woman who knows how to tell a story through images and words.

Raquel went to advertising school, and then landed some plum jobs in her industry. Success came fast for Raquel, and left her feeling a bit empty. After just a few years of agency life, she figured out that the traditional advertising career path wasn't for her.

Raquel struggled with the question of what to do next. Starting a family was on the horizon, and as she puts it, people in her field of work, "didn't know when they were going to get home at night." The long hours and what-have-you-done-for-me-lately culture of advertising wasn't appealing, but she wanted to stay connected to the creative side. Raquel says, "I think deep down, I just wanted something different. Something where I had more control." Sounds like a Mom Boss.

Untamed Studios plays to Raquel's strengths, because she uses photography and design to help build brands. Finding clients wasn't much of an issue. So many women in her network had ideas for businesses or had small brands that were already up-and-running. Raquel helped these companies develop into brands.

"These women needed to look professional, but they didn't have websites," Raquel says. Her clients were aiming to charge premium prices in industries like interior design, catering, and fashion. Raquel knew they needed a professional polish to turn a business idea into a stream of steady revenue.

When you are thinking about your brand, think big picture. You want the photography, logo, and website to reflect both what the brand is now, and also what it can become. "Most people that come to me have been playing at a business on the side. It's never fully figured out," Raquel says. Her job is to ask a million questions and get to the heart of the matter. Raquel serves as an advisor to many Mom Bosses setting up shop.

"I sit down with them, and talk about what they are doing and where they want to go. This helps me figure out how to brand them," Raquel says.

Don't wing it. Investing time and thought into your logo and website is essential. Hiring a professional is not a waste of money. Find an expert who knows your industry and don't be afraid to ask for revisions. You want to get this right.

Rachel's Logo Tips:

It's ok to have just a name, but do think about a five and ten-year plan. If you hope to grow your team, will using your name hold you back?

◊ Look for timeless fonts and colors.

◊ Look at your competitors, and try to stand out.

◊ Google everything. Do your research to make sure you can own your brand without conflict.

Just about every business is going to need a website; plan on $5,000 for an attractive, functional site. Keep in mind that e-commerce sites will cost you much more money to build out. Build in a budget for some professional photography too. At the very least, you want a great head shot to represent your brand on your site.

One warning from Raquel: the DIY website movement can be fraught with problems. Though services like Squarespace may look intuitive, they can't ensure that you match fonts and have consistent branding. When setting up your website, be sure to use these tips:

◊ **Keep colors consistent**

◊ **Keep font family consistent**

◊ **Keep names consistent**

Time for the last step: figuring out where you are going to work. The good news is, many Mom Bosses run the lion's share of their business from a smartphone, and don't need a physical space.

Leticia Barr runs the site techsavvymama.com out of her Maryland home. Her site is a trusted resource when it comes to education and technology. She makes money not only from sponsored work on her blog, but as a valued tech consultant. She can do most of her work from a laptop and smartphone.

Technology needs:

◊ **A smartphone with an excellent camera and lots of storage**

◊ **Hi-speed internet**

◊ **A laptop with good storage capacity**

◊ **A good backup system**

The first three things might be intuitive. Don't wait until a crisis occurs to develop your backup plan. Leticia advises using both cloud storage and an external hard drive. For many businesses, a home office like Leticia's is perfect. She has a dedicated office space that she can write-off for tax purposes. Other women may be able to work from the kitchen table and Starbucks. If you don't need an office, save yourself some money and work from home. Figure out both your budget and your work style. If you crave human interaction when the kids are away, look into shared desk space like We Work, or plan your days so that you can nab a table at your favorite cafe a few days a week.

For some moms, setting up shop means renting virtual space. For the majority of Etsy and eBay sellers, virtual commerce sites help them save thousands of dollars in rent.

Shauna Moore Thuet lives in Saint Louis, and runs a successful Etsy Shop called BOWQUETgifts. Shauna started her work life as a salon owner right out of Cosmetology School, but decided that she wanted to be a Mom Boss who works from home. She wanted to be there for her identical twin boys, Cance and Rylan, who are developmentally delayed.

Shauna came up with the idea for BOWQUET gifts with her daughter Keegan. Keegan had a best friend with extreme allergies, and wanted to make her a hair bow gift basket. Keegan said, "Mom, no one is allergic to PRETTY!"

Shauna says that when it comes to selling products and running a virtual shop, "everything is trial and error." Buying in bulk can save you money, and Shauna recommends matching your packaging to your brand. "You'd be surprised how decorative ribbon, tissue, and business cards in your own branded colors can give your packages that high-end look for pennies," Shauna says.

Instead of investing in rent, Shauna spends on SEO, photography, and market research. Since she doesn't get the chance to interact with her customers in person, she uses her website and social media to research what is working, and what isn't.

Emails are gold. Every entrepreneur knows this. To build a clientele, you're going to have to make your site and social media properties so attractive and engaging that customers will entrust their money and emails with you.

Shauna advises asking every single customer if you can add them to an email list to keep them up-to-date on sales and new merchandise. Shauna recommends having a link to join your mailing list in every thank you email after someone makes a purchase. A little incentive helps too. Shauna offers a 20 percent discount to new members on her mailing list.

Once you've got them on your list, Shauna advises to use it well. You'll want to contact your clients at least once a month to stay relevant, and never stop getting feedback. Look at every customer interaction as a chance to grow - especially when you are getting started.

What keeps Shauna motivated to keep doing better? She loves her work and she's got two little guys counting on her. 100 percent of the proceeds of BOWQUET gifts go towards Chance and Rylan's medical expenses. As she puts it: "Truly, this is cuteness with a CAUSE!" No matter what you're going to do with the profits, know that a solid start will help smooth the path to success.

NOTES

Chapter 10

GETTING ORGANIZED

Time to whip out your paper and pencils, ladies. This chapter is all about creating the ultimate to-do list for small business owners. I, for one, hate keynote speeches that are 99 percent inspiration and 1 percent actionable items.

TO IMPLEMENT CHANGE, YOU'VE GOT TO WORK. MOM BOSSES AREN'T JUST BIG TALKERS. THEY ARE BIG DOERS.

Figure Out How You are Going to Make Money

I've been working with Vicki Kosuda, a fellow Mom Boss and owner of Beyond Financials Consulting, for the past five years. Before kids, Vicki spent years working in a highly structured job in the financial sector. When she had her twins, she took two years off. Her next step was a return to work on a part-time basis working for a CFO. While many women would have been envious of her three-day-a-week schedule, she still felt like it was a poor compromise; "I was still missing a lot of things with my children."

Vicki decided that she was done having kids after the birth of her twins. This realization meant that every milestone was monumental to her. "I thought it was time for me to define how I want to work," Vicki says of why she became a Mom Boss.

Friends thought Vicki was crazy to give up a well-paying job. She knew better. Technology enabled her to be accessible and communicate with people across the country and around the world. She didn't need an office and nine-to-five in a cubical.

To build her business, she partnered with new accounting software companies like XERO (that's how I connected with Vicki, through a XERO referral). She also volunteered her time to do presentations at local business groups and networked online. Vicki continues to grow her company, working with clients like Momtrends who want an accountant who works differently. Because she's flexible, creative, and focused on results, she gets a slew of referrals.

I highly recommend finding an accountant like Vicki who speaks your Mom Boss language from the outset. Part of her generosity is sharing tools with startups.

Vicki says you need to start with a clean slate. That doesn't mean spending a ton on complicated legal fees at the beginning. It means documenting.

From the VERY start you need to open a separate bank account and separate credit card for your business. You don't need to be set up as an LLC for this. A basic business designation is a Sole Proprietor.

Once you have your accounts set up, you've got to keep financial records. Even if it's a simple Microsoft Excel spreadsheet, you need to know what you are starting with, and what you are spending. Your basic account will look something like this example for a professional blogger:

All money received goes into the sales bucket. All the money that goes out gets put in the expense bucket. What is left is your profit.

To get started, you'll need to deposit some startup capital ($) into your business account. Be sure to strictly limit personal expenses through the business. Ladies, it gets messy if you co-mingle funds. Keep things tidy. Don't buy things for your personal use on that credit card. Transfer your profits out of the business account and into your personal account to reap the rewards of your success. If you don't keep track of your numbers, you'll never know if you are becoming profitable.

Separating your business and personal life is also a means to protect yourself. When you co-mingle funds, you are opening your family up to risk. In addition to meeting with an accountant for advice, I also recommend a meeting with an insurance agent to look into liability insurance. Some homeowner's insurance policies cover at-home business, but don't assume anything.

When you make your first sale or sign your first deal, it's time to invoice (yes, you are allowed to do a little happy dance first).

SALES

Blogger Revenue	$50,000
Affiliate Revenue	$2,500
Event Revenue	$5,000

Total Sales $57,500

LESS: EXPENSES

Bank Fees	($125)
Conferences	($750)
Contractors	($2,000)
Events	($250)
Insurance	($500)
Legal & Professional Services	($750)
License Fees	($150)
Marketing & Promotion	($2,500)
Meals & Entertainment	($500)
Merchant Fees	($425)
Office Equipment	($1,500)
Office Space	($1,200)
Software	($500)
Supplies	($250)
Travel	($1,000)
Website (design/hosting)	($4,500)

Total Expenses ($16,900)

Profit $40,600

Goal= *Higher* Sales, *Lower* Expenses

Ideally, you haven't waited until this point to figure out how you are going to invoice. PayPal is easy at first, and so is FreshBooks (Vicki also recommends Xero, QuickBooks Online, and Wave). Vicki advises getting a system set up before you land your first contract. Vicki also suggests coming up with the payment terms. Are payments going to be due on invoice? Or will half be due upon signing a contract and half due upon completion?

As your business grows, you might want to set up an LLC. As our business was growing, I hired a lawyer to set up my LLC for about $500 (it's possible to do this yourself for less). Lawyers can also be useful for drawing up basic contracts for your business. Once it's set, you can use it as a template. There are also websites like LawDepot. com that can provide inexpensive resources.

Let's get back to the money. You need to <u>constantly monitor</u> your finances. I recommend setting aside one morning a week to follow up on invoicing and pay bills. Get a system for your paperwork in place from the start - try software from Shoeboxed or Receipt Bank, or you can scan everything and sort it by month. And yes, some Mom Bosses still use old school paper files. Just have a system in place so that you don't end up sifting through chaos at the end of the year.

As you are working, keep receipts to support business related expenses like travel, meals and entertainment, and asset purchases like computers, equipment, and furniture.

Keeping track of your spending will help you see if you have a profitable business. Don't fret if you end the year a bit short. Vicki says most businesses won't see a profit in the first year. By checking in with your progress, you can see where you need to adjust - maybe by raising prices or cutting back on spending. It's essential to keep up with the numbers. Vicki says, "You want to see the loss slowly going away. If the loss isn't gone in the second year, there's a problem."

One way to control costs is to work from home as long as possible. Vicki says you've really got to have a strong case to warrant the expense of renting a physical space. In the beginning phase of your business, all you need is wi-fi and a laptop. However, as samples come in and client meetings happen, you might need physical space. Inventory and rent are the two budget busters for new businesses. Manage them well.

If you are truly in need of an office space, tap into your network. You'd be surprised how many companies are willing to sublet a desk to help them save on rent. For instance, if you are starting a massage therapy business, ask your local gym or salon if you can rent a room from them. Be creative and frugal. For more traditional workspaces, look into the cool trend of co-working spaces like Green Desk and We Work. About a year ago, it was clear my team of 10 could no longer work out of my living room. Our business is now based out of We Work in DUMBO. They take care of cleaning, security, building insurance, and wifi - heck, they even provide the tea and coffee. Squeeze into the smallest space possible and grow as your revenues grow.

For outfitting your office, look for used items. We Work has a community board where businesses list equipment and furniture that is no longer need. It's amazing the stuff people are willing to GIVE away when they are downsizing or relocating.

If you are looking to set up a storefront, either physical or e-commerce, think small first. Before you sign a lease or design an expensive website, consider in-home trunk shows or selling your goods on eBay or Etsy. Other ideas on starting small include getting a booth or table at your child's Christmas bazaar, or at local art fairs where renting a table might only cost $150. In a nutshell, do everything you can on the cheap before you have to write the big checks. The benefit of starting small: you can learn from feedback before you launch into design.

If you are starting a business that requires physical inventory, make your initial order as small as possible. It's always better to sell out of something than to have thousands of extra onesies gathering dust in your living room.

Once you've done your homework, you can feel more confident signing a lease or hiring a web designer. This is when you <u>don't skimp</u>. Redoing a substandard website can be twice as expensive as starting with a great design.

Working solo is ideal while you are in your visionary mode. Vicki advises delaying hiring employees as long as possible. Employees require reams of paperwork, more insurance, and more income to cover salaries. If you can make due with a freelancer (otherwise known as a contractor), do it. I contract out web design, art projects, videography, and more.

When you do take the plunge and decide to hire someone, make sure you've got a year's worth of salary you can reliably fund. It's horrible to have to fire someone not because they aren't performing, but because you underestimated the expense. Vicki advises: "Your first person should always be part-time." That's what I did with our first editorial hire - she came on as a part-time editor. As business increased, I gave her a raise and more responsibility. Be honest about what you've got to offer, and where you see the business going. Remember, the odds are stacked against the entrepreneur. We'll talk more about this in the next chapter, but you'll need to keep records of everyone you hire. You collect a W-9 and issue a 1099 at the end of the year.

Here's the good news about this careful approach to spending: Vicki sees a lot more of her female clients succeed. "Women self-fund and go slower," Vicki says. "Men tend to go for venture capital funding, hire big, and opt for a lot of bells and whistles with what they are creating." She thinks this is why more male businesses fail.

Structuring your work day is as important as structuring your business. Nina Restieri of MomAgenda knows what it's like to be pulled in many directions. Nina is the Founder of MomAgenda, and a mom of four.

In 2005, she launched MomAgenda. Her company started with a single great product, an original day planner created for mothers.

MomAgendas are both stylish and functional. They help women eliminate the chaos of mom life.

Nina wants to help other Mob Bosses succeed by helping them stay on task. She remembers the early years "where you're creating something out of nothing. Sometimes it felt like rolling a boulder up a hill. I had no idea how hard it would be."

Now she uses her MomAgenda to stay on top of things. Like many Moms Bosses, she didn't start with a plan; she started with solving a problem. Once she figured out the solution, she worked out a business to make it profitable.

Nina works out of her home office in Connecticut. It's chicly decorated with a white furry rug, fireplace, white desk, and pink zebra chair. It is a fabulous reflection of her brand, MomAgenda. Each Sunday, she sits down with her planner to schedule in her priorities. Her tip: "Schedule in your breaks. If naps are important to you, schedule those in too! The only way to ensure you have time for something is to schedule it, and treat it like the important appointment it is." For Nina, this means carving out time to run.

Since you're a Mom Boss, you've got to worry about things like feeding the family, too. Nina devises a master meal list with all of her go-to recipes for healthy family means. She shops and plans for the week, picking five meals from the master list. Nina says to "take into account which nights you'll be picking up kids late from school or going to games, so you can schedule in easy meals for those nights."

Brooke Stewart is the Founder of Power Moms Media. She serves as a talent agent of sorts, connecting brands with online influences. Brooke is the mom of two boys, and has represented Momtrends for the past seven years. In that time, she has landed me millions of dollars in work, and been an inspiration to me is so many ways. She's tremendously creative about finding time to work. I love the attitude she brings to our collaborations. I never feel she's distracted or rushed, so I had to get some of her tips.

"A few years ago, I made a conscious decision to stop feeling guilty. I was letting work and Mom Guilt get the best of me. We think we need to do it all, but doing it all comes at a big price," Brooke says.

She was getting frazzled trying to be present with her kids at every moment and run a business. "I remember taking a client call while at my neighborhood pizza place, and my newly potty-trained son yells out that he has to go number two. I spent the call running in and out of the bathroom. I managed to close the deal, but that was more stressful than any business deal I had done in my previous (no-kid) life," Brooke retells.

She made a conscious shift in how she works and parents. Her focus now is quality of time vs. sheer quantity. When she first started her business, Brooke felt the need to say yes to everything so that she didn't miss out on any opportunities. "It didn't take long to realize that not every event or meeting is worth taking. I've learned to ask the right questions and take the time to vet things before saying yes," Brooke says. With some well-earned wisdom, Brooke has some self-imposed limits: "I say no to client calls or emails between getting home from work at 6 p.m. and putting my kids to bed at 9 p.m."

Brooke is also trying to limit multitasking. "I try to spend an hour or two with the boys each day where we are all unplugged. This is more valuable to me than what I was doing before - constantly yelling at them to 'give me a minute.' That old way wasn't fair to any of us," Brooke says.

Like Nina, Brooke is intentional about engineering her calendar to get the most out of her work hours. She works out right after school drop-off (and I must say, a theme for many of the most successful Mom Bosses is that they make time for exercise). "As hard as I try, I cannot be in two places at once. My scheduling certainly has to get creative." Thanks to personal hotspots and a wifi portal built into her phone package, she can work just about anywhere. "Waiting rooms, in my car, at soccer tournaments, the coffee shop near my kids' school - you name it. I know which subway stops have wifi, and where I can hop off to make a conference call," Brooke says.

Most Friday afternoons, Brooke takes off early from work to spend time with her boys. "It's the one-day where they don't have activities or a sitter, and we can relax together." As a Mom Boss, she's figured out ways to make her business work for her.

With school-age kids, loads of friends, and a growing business, she gets asked to attend a lot of events. "Having my own business does give me the luxury of having my own time. I can re-arrange my schedule to be at school events or soccer games," Brooke says. Here's how she prioritizes: Brooke says "yes" if it's something she feels will get her closer to closing a deal with a client or if it's something important to her family or close friends. Anything else has to be justified as a draw on her time and babysitting budget.

That's an important reminder: Mom Bosses need to factor in child care costs into the business model. Babysitting can add up and eat at the profits. If you're only making $1,500 a month in profit but spending $1000 on child care, you'll have to ask yourself if it is worth it.

Don't forget to ask for help. Brooke says, "I'm also lucky to have a friend in the building who works in the public school system. I help take her kids to school in exchange for her picking up or watching my kids on evenings I have an event or meeting." This swapping system works well for single moms. If you've got a partner at home, be sure to split duties. Brooke and her husband swap watching the boys when they have evening events - they share a Google calendar to make planning easier. Finally, I love her last tip: "Back-off of signing the kids up for too much stuff." Just like we do, kids need a little down time.

NOTES

_____

_____

_____

_____

_____

_____

_____

_____

_____

_____

_____

Chapter 11

FIND YOUR TRIBE

While you may think that a startup can be lonely, in fact, smart Mom Bosses are never alone. We have tribes. What is a tribe? It's the women who work for you, your mentors, and your customers/clients.

Fortunately for Mom Bosses, women are really, really good at starting tribes. While they may lack the gumption to ask for seed money, they know how to make connections and help one another out. As a mom, you've got an asset that is extremely valuable to your startup: you've got a mom network.

When you became a mother, you joined a very inclusive club. You know how it is; moms have each other's backs. Ever been stuck at a playground without a back-up diaper and wipes? Yep, so have I. And there was always someone there to lend me a wipe and a changing mat, and giggle with me about the situation. Mom friends share snacks when we forget to pack them, and they help with drop-off when we've got a work meeting. Your friends want you to succeed; so let them. Use the willing as focus groups, advisors, and mentors. And yes, ask them to become customers, too.

Mentors and Advisors

First, let's talk about finding mentors. Since female entrepreneurship is a fairly recent trend, there aren't scads of us to go around. But I find that those women who <u>have</u> launched successful companies are usually generous with their time.

In fact, the best multi-level marketing teams have powerful, generous, female mentors at the top of the sales force. Through their training and sharing, they are able to help their new team members find success. Paying it forward is in the Mom Boss's DNA.

Sometimes a mentor can be a peer; a fellow entrepreneur in the throes of startup mode. Having a friend who is going through the process with you makes the startup roadblocks less challenging. She'll know when to challenge your decisions and be there to toast your success.

Usually, the best mentors have some experience to share and are generous with imparting wisdom. At Momtrends, we've started a "Business of Blogging Series." It's a quarterly get-together of professional women who are looking to turn their blogs into brands. We gather industry experts like accountants, graphic designers, and professional photographers to give the attendees tips and training. We don't make a profit on these events (in fact we barely cover our costs), but it's the right thing to do - and an awesome way to give back.

You can find mentors through family, church, community groups, and on the soccer sidelines. Social media (Facebook and LinkedIn) is also a terrific place to find mentors.

Once you've identified your mentor or advisor, it's time for the rules of networking and marketing. You can master the art of the networking coffee date if you mind your Ps:

◊ **Propose:** Email or call with an offer to buy your contact coffee or tea. Lunch is too big of a time commitment for a first date. Pick a spot that is convenient for her, not you. Make it logistically easy for her to meet you. And yes, you should pick up the tab.

◊ **Prep:** Dazzle her with your preparation. Read up on her business. Have one concrete complement to share. It's rude to go in just blindly knowing that she's generally successful.

◊ **Prioritize:** Come to the meeting with one concrete problem you want to solve or connection you want to make. You are not there for a general brain picking. Be focused.

◊ **Be Polite and Prompt:** Be on time, dress professionally, and be gracious. Say thank you for her time with a handwritten note or email. Ask for permission to keep her in the loop about your progress.

Let me walk you through a coffee date timeline:

◊ **5 minutes greeting:** This is where you compliment her.

◊ **1-2 minute** elevator pitch of your business: This is where you SUCCINCTLY explain where you are in the process, and the specific area you need help in.

◊ **20 minutes** listening and asking questions: Remember, this isn't a monologue; you're there to listen to her.

◊ **5 minutes** recapping what was discussed and laying out action plans.

◊ Thank her for her time, and give her an easy exit.

Trust me. If you follow these steps, there's a 90 percent chance of a second meeting.

When you call or email to set up the coffee date, make it clear that you have a business-related conversation in mind. It's not fair to blindside her with a pitch if she thinks you're going to be dishing about school gossip.

Be specific about your questions. This is not the time to say, "I'm thinking of starting a business. Can you help me?" This is a waste of her time, and yours.

Sample Email:

Hi Marni,

Hope you've recovered from the rainy game last weekend. I'm still drying out little Jade's cleats.

I have a favor to ask: I know you're incredibly busy, but I am so impressed with your work as the VP of Merchandise at Blooming-dales. I'm starting a new bedding brand called Sweet Dreams & Jelly Beans. I just got my first production samples back, and I'm looking to get some professional feedback. Can I pry you away from your work for a mid-day coffee break?

What have you accomplished? She knows it's going to be business. She knows you're prepared. She knows you have something in development already. In a nutshell, you've made it easy for her to say yes.

I get asked for a lot of "brain picking" sessions. How horrible! For me, the more vague the request, the less likely I am to say yes. If it's a specific ask, I feel well-equipped to say yes or no. Then, if someone is willing to come to me for 30 minutes and make it easy on my schedule, I'm 90 percent more likely to say yes.

More networking rules on your first meeting: Don't ask for money, and don't ask for all her contacts.

Building Your Team

Another tribe you're going to need is your support staff. In the beginning, this may be freelancers, virtual assistants, photographers, accountants, and designers. However, eventually you may need actual employees.

When your business becomes too big for you to manage alone, you've got to draft your dream team. Lawson Harris is a fitness maven and Mom Boss. A former professional dancer, she starred on Broadway and toured with elite dance companies before starting her pilates business.

In a very competitive industry, Lawson stands out for her work ethic and business smarts. She knows how to find a tribe and keep them happy. Her studio has a devoted clientele - some might even call them groupies - and a dedicated and motivated staff. It all started with demanding excellence.

When Lawson retired from Broadway to start a family, she moved to Westchester, NY and set up her first pilates studio in her home. She'd done her research. She knew her clientele would be stay-at-home moms who needed to fit workouts between school hours. "I set up the studio to work around them," says Lawson. By staying attuned to what her clients wanted, and when they wanted to work out, she grew her business.

Word of mouth helped Lawson grow to the point where she was able to open her first studio. Then, two more quickly followed. Fifteen years later, she runs a boutique pilates studio in DUMBO Brooklyn - one of New York City's trendiest neighborhoods. Her private workout sessions go for $100 an hour.

From the beginning, Lawson built her business with mom-friendly hours. She set up her work life so that she could serve her customers and train her employees all during the school day, leaving her evenings free to be with her kids. To cover the other hours, Lawson needed a strong team she could trust with her hard-earned clientele.

Since eight out of every ten **gyms fail** in the first five years, Lawson knew she needed to have high standards from the start. When she couldn't find ideal employees, she concocted a plan to train her own. (If you can't find your tribe, make your tribe!) She started a pilates instructor certification class. The idea was, she would find raw talent, train them, and supply herself with quality fitness professionals. Mom Bosses know if you want something done right, you do it yourself.

In her pilates course, Lawson teaches the students how to perform and instruct all the standard pilates exercises - plus a lot more. Lawson is not only educating her students on how to become strong pilates instructors, she's teaching them how to run a business.

All the applicants to her program have to meet her standards of fitness and professionalism. Being picky pays off. Lawson invests a lot of man hours into each student; in return, they give her a small deposit and sweat equity. They help around the studio, assist with classes, answer phones, maintain equipment, and interact with customers. They get a 360° view of what it means to run a studio. Lawson is teaching them how to succeed, not just do a perfect circus freak (it's a pilates exercise). "Every employee you hire has to reflect well on you. Hire slowly, and you won't regret it," Lawson says.

When she's training instructors, she gives them respect. In return, they reward her with dedication.

"You can't have a bad day," Lawson says, because her "kids" (the young students) pick-up on everything she does. "Leave your personal drama at the door and dress the part," Lawson says.

Remember: your tribe is going to be attracted to your energy. You'll never see Lawson on the street in schlumpy sweats. She's dressed to work out, but also looks like she could go out. "You are your brand," says Lawson. Especially if you run a bricks and mortar operation; you need to be ready to meet your next customer on the street.

She treats her staff and her customers with positivity, professionalism, and loads of encouragement. When you walk into The Fit Lab, you don't slouch. You wear cute gym clothes, work your buns off, and feel awesome afterwards. Never forget that as a Mom Boss, you personify your brand. Lawson's toned body inspires a lot of her clients. At 50, she makes her 20-year-old students envious of her form. "If I didn't look good, I would be embarrassed to be their leader," Lawson says. Keeping her tribe happy has given her career longevity, and helped her stand apart from the noisy fitness marketplace.

Word of Mom

Morgan Hutchinson had a problem: after she gave birth to her daughter, she struggled to find designer clothes that fit her new mom life. "90 percent of my closet wasn't working for me after my daughter Olive was born," Morgan says. Before Olive was born, Morgan worked in fashion. Suddenly, she was settling in after a move from Hong Kong back to the United States, breastfeeding, and networking to figure out her next career move. Her life was beautifully full, but her clothes couldn't seem to keep up. As a style maven, she scoured shops and online stores for clothes that worked for her.

One of the most specific fashion challenges was finding tops that worked for breastfeeding moms. "Mom life presented different challenges and different needs from my wardrobe," Morgan says. Surely, she couldn't be the only fashionista mama with this problem?

The solution was ShopBuru.com, an e-commerce boutique for new and expecting moms. Morgan is about to celebrate three years in business, and her site is still going strong. In those three years, Morgan has expanded her reach and become a trusted style source for moms who otherwise might not have access to clothes that fit their aesthetics and their busy lives.

Standing out was the toughest challenge for Morgan. There are millions of websites out there competing for a new mom's attention. How was she going to get her small, online boutique to make a big splash?

The key for Morgan was starting with a ripple.

Once Morgan made her first wholesale purchases and set up her website for business, she slowly and purposefully got feedback. "It was completely grassroots. I started with 20 of my friends who were new moms. I used a tool I knew I had… friends and Facebook," Morgan says.

Unlike most business owners, Morgan didn't just get feedback, she listened to it and quickly implemented change. She reached out to her friends and made them a beta testing group.

"Make sure you are willing to evolve and adjust based on feedback," Morgan says. For example, one of the first 20 women to test the site said that Morgan should use PayPal as a payment option. It was an involved process to get the PayPal portal setup, and Morgan wasn't sure it would matter. But rather than ignore the feedback, she dove in and figured out how to get PayPal connected. And wouldn't you know it? A huge portion of sales on ShopBuru are facilitated by PayPal.

After the initial 20 friends tested the site, Morgan widened the circle. She graduated from the University of Alabama and was in a sorority. She was closely connected to many of them on Facebook, And 90 percent of them had young children at home or were starting families.

One week before she went live, she sent the beta site to 50 more people from her Facebook inner circle with a personal note. Every single friend opened the link, and everyone gave her feedback. Once the site was live, she kept widening the circle, and asking for referrals. Her first 900 customers were from her Facebook community.

It wasn't just that Morgan had a good eye and good contacts; she knew how to give her tribe what they needed. She found chic pants from designers with elastic waists for moms who weren't quite back to their pre-baby size, or tops that were easy pop open to breast-feed. She found up-and-coming designers like Mara Hoffman who were underrepresented in boutiques and department stores. She also kept a close eye on customer service.

Rather than hiring a big expensive PR campaign, she focused on her friends and serving their needs. "Our whole mindset is that we want to make mom's life easier," Morgan says.

Morgan also figures out a way to leverage her contacts into clever marketing. ShopBuru calls it the Tastemaker program. Morgan wanted to feature women doing incredible things in their careers as content for the ShopBuru blog. Tastemakers is an exclusive Q & A with a mom who is also a social media maven.

"We started Tastemakers really early on. Two weeks into launching, we featured our first one," Morgan says. Each Tastymaker gives a brief interview and provides a photo or two, but they also do one more thing... they curate selections from ShopBuru for a Tastemaker wish list. Morgan came up with this genius idea. The Tastemakers help sell products because they have excellent taste. By selecting 10-15 items from the site, they are in effect putting their stamp of approval on those ten items - And it never costs Morgan a dime.

"We don't expect or demand that our tastemakers share the interview on social media. But 95 percent of them do re-share," Morgan says. All those shares are business referrals - and a way to grow your tribe.

Morgan works out of her Salt Lake City home, and she's thrilled with the slow and steady pace. "My path might not be that fast, but that's ok; I've got amazing customers," Morgan says. Morgan reminds herself that being a Mom Boss "is a marathon, not a sprint." She believes in staying nimble, dreaming big, and starting small. Small is beautiful when you've got a passionate tribe.

A word about social media etiquette. Of course it's ok to use social media to promote your brand - but make it only a PART of your social media imprint. Make sure your feed is more than selling. Follow the 80/20 rule. 80 percent of your posts should be informative, and 20 percent can be promotional.

Here's an example on how to use Facebook.
An interior designer might post:

1. A link to a cool article about home staging

2. A link to a great sale on outdoor furniture

3. A garden shot of an azalea bush with a tip about watering

4. A link to a recipe you just tried for a terrific slow cooker fajita

5. A share from a friend's page who is hosting a yard sale this weekend

6. A share from Buzzfeed about lemurs doing yoga (just 'cause it's funny)

7. A share from HGTV about the new season's line-up

8. An article about home sale prices in your county

9. A link to an article featuring your work

10. A link to your last blog post about the five way to spruce up a powder room for under $100

You see how this works? All the posts are related and relevant but not a constant stream of ask, ask, ask. You've got to give. Be generous and human. And for goodness sake, use your like button liberally. Comment away on other people's feeds on Snapchat, Instagram, YouTube, and Facebook.

Chapter 12

KNOW YOUR WORTH

A s a mom boss you've got to get comfortable with some degree of risk-taking. You also have to believe in yourself: It's your dream, and it's time to own it. No one is going to buy from you or invest in you if you're not "all in."

Liana Buonanno is the Co-founder of Gooseneck Vineyards, and serves as President at the Wickford Wine Company. Before heading up her wine business, Liana was an investment banker. When large corporations would run into financial trouble, she would go in to help them either by raising funds or helping the company through bankruptcy.

There was no particular straw that broke the camel's back that made Liana leave her finance career. "It was more of a gradual shift of priorities. I noticed myself not wanting to go to work too often after my first son was born," Liana says. She made a drastic career shift – from the boardroom to the vineyards.

Now she works out of her two home offices; one in Rhode Island, and the other in New York City, devoting her talents to Gooseneck Vineyards. The name comes from a cove on Narragansett Bay, where her family shared vacations. Her company goal is to transport her customers "to the beaches of the beautiful Narragansett Bay" as they sip her wines. She had confidence in her vision for the company. She knew which grapes would grow well on the East Coast, and set her mind to developing an "award-winning Prosecco and Pinot Grigio." She used what she had – a love of wine and financial acumen – to start a vineyard.

Confidence sells wine – and it also brings investors. If you don't have a believable elevator pitch, you better get one, fast. The stakes are high. Liana employs people that depend on her vision. The hardest part of her job is: "Feeling the responsibility for everyone involved in the business. If the business doesn't do well, everyone suffers."

Get Comfortable with a Little Chaos

"I have a desk in our guest room in NY that is always full of papers, stacked in an organized fashion (only to me)," Liana says. Mom Bosses have to let go of the belief that all aspects of life are going to be picture perfect. Your priorities are your family and your work. Your time is best served on one of these two things - especially when you are in startup mode.

ASK YOURSELF - WHAT ARE YOU WILLING TO SACRIFICE TO MAKE YOUR DREAMS COME TRUE?

For Liana, deep REM sleep is a luxury. "The biggest daily sacrifice is sleep," Liana says. "Running a business, and your family, leaves you in a constant sleep deprived state,"

Mom Bosses must be very focused on their priorities - but the choices aren't easy. For Liana, she misses out on time with girlfriends. "The business is seven days a week, and so is being a mom. I used to go away with my girlfriends every year for at least four days to Italy. That had to stop." This makes it even more important to hire people who are not only competent and committed, but who will become part of your work family.

Define Your Success Early

Write down your goals and look at them often. For Liana, it's not just about the money: "Success is having the ultimate flexibility - financial and personal."

Liana advises that you develop thick skin quickly. "The wins feel great and the setbacks, no matter how little, hurt a lot," Liana says. "I was told that in order to run a business, you have to be prepared for the huge up and down emotional swings. I thought that in any job or even at home, we always have ups and downs. But the way they are processed internally is very different when you have a startup."

Figure out a way to celebrate the wins and find a tribe to help you through those rough patches. For Liana, this means maintaining a great network of friends and fellow entrepreneurs. With them, she can share all the joys, and during the rough patches, these same people remind her that one failure is not cataclysmic. "Someone once pointed out a comparison to me that as an entrepreneur, we are working in the forest among the trees all the time. So when a tree almost falls on us, it's very frightening. However, as soon as we have a bird's eye view of the forest, one fallen tree doesn't mean much," Liana says.

Remember to share your goals with your family. Let them know there might be less money for splashy vacations but there will be more QMT (Quality Mom Time). Liana says, "It is so important that everyone is on the same page when it comes to starting a business. The hurdles to overcome can be enormous, and without constant support, it's very easy to give up." If your family is behind your dreams, that helps a lot.

Perfect Timing Doesn't Exit

For many Mom Bosses, there will never be the perfect time to start a company. Leaving the security of work takes some planning, and sometimes a karmic nudge. Bo Arlander, Co-founder of Moxie Capital, became a Mom Boss relatively late, but she's making up for lost time.

"When you have kids, things change," Bo Arlander says. Bo lives in San Francisco, and became a single mom at age 43. Before becoming a Mom Boss, she spent 11 years at Bear Stearns Merchant Banking in an extremely competitive and male dominated industry.

In her old life, Bo would get up at 4:30 a.m. to pump breast milk for her baby. She'd leave her house at 5:30 a.m. to get in her triathlon workout, and be at her desk by 7:30 a.m. Bo would then put in a full day working with her NY team on new investment opportunities and portfolio company matters. After an 11-hour workday, Bo would head home to sneak in some quality time with Mirabel before she went to bed. Then she'd start it all over again the next day. Did I mention she had to fly to New York every couple of weeks too?

Time off was elusive in her industry. Bo's team was all about chasing the next big deal. The one thing that was sacred on her calendar was a week in Hawaii for the Ironman World Championship.

"I was running myself ragged," Bo says. She promised herself things would change now that she was a mom. She'd put in 17 years of corporate life on Wall Street, and had nothing left to prove. She'd long ago become financially secure (which, for a single mom, is a huge concern) by investing her bonuses and profit sharing dollars wisely.

The big question was: What to do next? Bo's chosen industry, private equity, had few women in it. No one showed her the path she should take. She had to make it up as she went along.

After JPMorgan took over Bear Stearns in 2008, Bo got her chance. She could have moved back to New York and thrown herself into more private equity work and closed more deals – or she could leave and do her own thing.

Bo opted to become a Mom Boss. First, she took some time off to network and research her next move. Bo teamed up with Lauren Cooks Levitan (mom of three), who was also at a crossroads. The two women formed Moxie Capital in January 2009. It was a firm that aimed at investing in consumer – facing businesses that either needed money to grow and thrive, or where an ownership change was desired. Moxie Capital operates as an independent sponsor; they find interesting investment opportunities and then bring them to family offices looking for companies to invest in.

It was an entirely new way of doing business. Lauren and Bo were 100 percent there for one another. Bo learned that closing deals could not only be lucrative and exciting, it could also be really fun. With a partner who also valued family, Bo never had to apologize for wanting to be 100 percent present for Mirabel. When family issues popped up, one or the other woman would compensate. Having a partner who had her back made all the difference: "I had so much more flexibility as to how I set my schedule," Bo says.

Eventually, Lauren left the partnership to take another opportunity. Bo shifted her focus from investing in well-established and growing brands, to angel investing. Now, her main goal is to help entrepreneurs by offering advice, investing in their companies, and introducing them to other potential investors. "I've come to a very secure place in my career. I don't need to close a certain number of deals a year," Bo says. Now she's got the luxury to help growing brands by sharing her years of experience and asking the tough questions. She's using her experience to not only make money, but to help the next generation of entrepreneurs be successful in launching and growing their companies.

Bo says there isn't a job offer with enough zeros in it to lure her back to work for someone else. "Slowing down and doing things on my own terms is a blessing," Bo says. "Leaving my old way of life has probably added ten years back to my life." Now, Bo gets to see her daughter every morning and attend swim practices, ballet rehearsals, and all the juicy stuff of motherhood. And she can still lock up a deal and service her fund if the right opportunity presents itself. Mom Bosses know that deals will come and go, but there's only one first recital.

Mom Boss Code of ResponsibilityDon't pull the ladder up with you. Once you attain success in your career, become a mentor and help others. Bo serves on several boards, shares her knowledge, and believes in angel investing.

Help a sister out. As a Mom Boss, you know all too well what it's like to have to ask permission to attend a school play. Make sure you "have the back" of the mom who is a corporate lawyer.

Make the most of your time. For Bo, this means attending events with her daughter, contributing at her daughter's school in various ways, and continuing to compete at the highest level in Ironman triathlons. Her current motto: "Life is short; make the most of each and every day!"

It's All About Confidence

The sooner you start believing that you deserve success, the better. Interior designer, Lindy Blake, was lucky. From a young age, her father coached her to succeed. She never doubted she would have a rich, fulfilling work life.

Lindy has been running her successful design firm (Blakedale Interiors + Haymarket Accessories) from the North Shore of Chicago for more than three decades. The secret to her success: Quitting just isn't an option.

Lindy was raised by an architect who insisted that his daughter have a career. While this might be standard now, it certainly wasn't the norm when Lindy was in high school and college. "My father told me 'you have to have a career, and your own money and freedom' and I listened," Lindy says.

Now, she's incredibly glad she did. Lindy has a Masters in Art, and a degree interior design. She started as a Solo Artist designing clubhouses for golf course, and now works with a partner and focuses mostly on residential interiors. As an empty-nester (she has three grown children), her life is more vibrant than ever. Lindy sees some of her peer group floundering. "When the kids went to college, these women were lost" Lindy says, referring to the women who decided to take time off while raising kids.

No matter how much money a spouse can bring to the table, Lindy believes women need to work. "You gain so much confidence from work," Lindy says - and her career wasn't just for show. "I had to work from a financial standpoint; I paid for all three kids to go to college." She needed to figure out a way to do what she loved, and make money from it.

Value Your Time

Dealing with unpaid invoices and collections is a part of being a Mom Boss. Lindy has an extraordinary track record for getting paid for her efforts, and she shares her tips.

MomBoss Tips for Getting Paid

Set the scope: When Lindy gets a call from a new client, she sets up a call or in-person meeting. At this meeting, Lindy gets copious details from the potential client. She takes notes and asks a TON of questions. Researching the scope of the work will prevent surprises down the road.

Present a written estimate: With her partner, Lindy figures out how the project will break down – what portion of the fees will come from new furniture commissions, and what will come from an hourly rate. Lindy presents her clients with a very clear description of what is included in the estimate. The more details you can cover in the estimate, the fewer things there are to quibble over at the end.

Obtain a sign off: The client must agree in writing to the scope and estimate. A verbal agreement is hard to manage. At the very least, get an email confirmation of your price.

Be honest: Lindy says, "It's really important to be transparent in the beginning. We reiterate the rates again and again so there are no surprises." If you feel like your client doesn't have the budget to work with you, it's ok to turn the project down or decrease the scope of the work. Setting clear, fair, and understandable rates will make you look more professional.

Deliver the goods: When you deliver excellent quality on time and with a smile, you are much more likely to get prompt payment.

Lindy says, "We've never had a complaint about a bill, and I've been doing this for 30 years." When you add fair pricing to an excellent product, you can't go wrong.

Being a Mom Boss is a great way to stay young and engaged. "I'm not getting rich from my work, but I'm going to do it for as long as I'm able. I truly enjoy helping people, and it feels good," Lindy says.

Lindy and her partner set themselves apart from the competition by being generous. "We never come into someone's home and judge," Lindy says. "We have a reputation for being really loving and accepting. We make people feel good about themselves."

Lindy is optimistic about helping quite a few more generations turn a house into a well-appointed home. She's also generous with younger designers. She often mentors younger up-and-coming designers, and is always there to lend a hand to someone looking into design as a career. "I find that women are eager to help other women get off the ground," Lindy says. Sharing has served Lindy well. She's never had to fret over her next job; her confidence and generosity seem to bring work into her orbit.

It hasn't always been easy to nurture a family and a business, but Lindy has no regrets. As she looks back on the years when the kids were little and life was more hectic, she says she's so glad she attempted to juggle it all.

Chapter 13

Mom Bosses know there is a lesson to be learned from every loss. As a wise ski coach once told me:

IF YOU'RE NOT FALLING OCCASIONALLY, IT MEANS YOU AREN'T TRYING HARD ENOUGH.

I want to put this on the table: As a Mom Boss, you are going to make mistakes. How you recover from those mistakes will define you, maybe even more than your successes.

Hope is Not a Strategy

I wish I could tell you that being a successful Mom Boss is all about hard work and great ideas. Sometime, you need a little luck and timing on your side, too. Mom Bosses are nimble and need to know when to pivot.

You've got to read the tea leaves. Make time in your work to analyze what is working and what isn't. Five years into my business, banner advertising all but dried up. In the beginning of our business, banner ads were a significant source of revenue. As I saw the numbers decline, I didn't chase the scraps of banner ads still available. Instead, I started to build up a new business segment called the Momtrends Blogger Outreach. Through this program, we connect brands with other bloggers for paid blog posts. While we took some early losses on this program to build the business, by diversifying our revenue streams, we were ultimately able to grow our business when other online publishers were feeling a pinch. If I hadn't taken the time to analyze what was going on, I might have missed an opportunity.

Relying on a Team

Pam Ginocchio and Melisa Fluhr have been friends since college. After graduation, they stayed close friends. When they started their families, they commiserated about scarcity of resources for aesthetically minded parents. They were experts at ferreting out the most desirable nursery goods. The duo decided to share knowledge and resources with other moms. Project Nursery was born. Now, their website gets millions of visitors a month and is THE go-to resource for parents planning dreamy (and functional) nurseries.

Along the way to building a million-dollar brand that now boasts a profitable e-commerce site, the ladies have managed to have more children, stay married, and foster a beautiful friendship. They are the first to tell you that it's not always pretty, and the road to success is littered with mistakes. The key is that Pam and Melisa study their mistakes, and don't make the same one twice.

FOMO Syndrome

FOMO = Fear of Missing Out. For an online publisher, it's easy to look around at what someone else is doing successfully and try to replicate it. Pam says, "It's easy to get distracted in this business; we call it squirrel syndrome, where we get attracted by shiny new things." While they may spend a moment chasing a new social media tool, the duo has learned that for them, they have to do a little analysis before they jump into a new opportunity.

What else doesn't work? Trying to be everything to everyone. "We are so niche," Melisa says. At its core, the site is about nursery design. When they drift far from this editorially or with brand partnerships, things start to unravel. "We just keep circling back to what we do best," Pam says. That's why expecting moms love them, and why brands get tremendous value working with them. All Mom Bosses can learn from this.

REMEMBER WHY YOU STARTED, WHO YOU SERVE, AND STAY TRUE TO THAT ORIGINAL MISSION.

Research shows that 80 percent of business partnerships fail. If you are thinking about bringin g a friend along on the Mom Boss ride, be sure you know what you are getting into, and take these tips from Pam and Melissa.

How to Keep a Partnership from Failing

Clearly define roles. You don't want to be on top of each other every day. For Pam and Melisa, their roles are clear, and there's a lot of geography between them; Pam is based in San Francisco, and Melisa is in New Jersey. Pam oversees editorial, partnerships, and PR. Melisa watches over the retail sales and the tech team.

Communicate. Don't hold in your feelings. Share your thoughts and, in return, listen to the concerns and needs of your partner.

Have aligned interests. Melisa and Pam have agreed to continually re-invest profits into the business. Before you launch a partnership, map out how the next few years will look in a number of scenarios. Are you on the same page when it comes to what to do if your business keeps missing certain goals?

Competition is Not so Flattering

Thanks to early success, the duo had many imitators. Nursery blogs were popping up everywhere. How would they set themselves apart? Pam and Melisa took a risk and invested $50,000 into new technology to create a virtual photo gallery on their site. The gallery allows readers to submit pictures and tell their personal nursery design story. The submissions rolled in, and the ladies got great content without having to do much work. The work was in the design of the new platform, and in spotting what the community was craving.

"That investment changed everything," Pam says. Pam and Melisa were leading, not watching, what others were doing. You've got to give yourself the space and time to be a visionary for your brand. "We are always trying to stay ahead of the curve," Melisa says. If you're too bogged down in the day-to-day minutia of your brand, you won't be able to look up and ahead.

It's a fine balance, the ladies say. "No one is going to care about your brand more than you do." The key for them is to never feel completely comfortable; when the ladies feel stretched a little thin and are slightly nervous, they know they are in a good spot.

Experimentation and risk are part of being a Mom Boss. Two years ago, Pam and Melisa started thinking about adding an e-commerce division to their business. The first inventory investments were some Chiapas dolls from a Mexican vendor. Now, the pair has more than 2000 skus in their e-shop.

At first, the ladies place bets on quantities by relying on knowledge of their customer and keen eye for product to fill the shop. Now a little wiser, they have an employed strategic buyer.

"We made the mistake of making emotional decisions, saying 'oh we just love this bedding, we have to buy it,'" Pam says. Gut instinct told them to buy big into some pretty toddler bedding that still sits in inventory a year later. Savvy Mom Bosses admit mistakes and fix them. They hired a strategic planner to help with inventory.

Learning to Say No

One of the hardest lessons for them to learn: their time is worth money. The ladies have had to learn how to say 'NO.'

A few years ago, they were lured into a brand partnership that didn't feel right from the beginning. "We were promised tremendous 'exposure' from a large and powerful baby gear brand, but never asked the right questions," Melisa says.

They leapt at the opportunity to work with a much larger brand in the hope that it would work out. They were promised tremendous "exposure." They undervalued the power of their brand in negotiations. It led to months of travel, and time spent away from family and the core business. Lesson learned. "It was a disaster," Pam says.

When a Deal Looks Too Good to be True, Ask These Questions

◊ Will this deal help my brand?

◊ If I am not getting a great monetary deal, will the exposure help me?

◊ What is the time commitment?

◊ Is the time and effort required from this deal going to take me away from my core business?

Get a written agreement. Verbal promises mean nothing at the end of the day. Always ask yourself if the deal will be moving your brand forward. "If a project takes us away from our core business, we have to turn it down," Pam says.

Asking for Help

Here are some of the life lessons I've learned. When we started Momtrends almost a decade ago, I had no idea I was going to build a blogger database, or need a system to track our client contacts. As our company grew, we amassed loads of contacts that fit into different buckets. We had email addresses for readers, email addresses for blogging friends, and email addresses for business contacts. My team and I used a patchwork system of Excel spreadsheets, email contact lists, and an email marketing tool to house all these contacts. It was a jumbled mess. Whenever we wanted to send a group invite, announcement, or marketing pitch, we had to cut and paste - it was quite inefficient.

Last year I hired a consultant to make order of our emails. In all, the project cost me $15,000. Had I put a system in place from the beginning, I would have saved myself thousands and thousands of dollars.

Mining for Gold

Your email list and contact list is gold. Treat it as such. From the beginning, have a tool to sort and record your contacts. This is a great place to hire a virtual assistant or (VA). VAs work for relatively low-cost wages, since they mostly work from home and only need a computer and phone to work. They are adept at data entry, mailings, and managing emails. Setting aside $100 a week to have an assistant work on your contacts is money well spent.

Give Them What They Want

Many entrepreneurs fall in love with their first idea. I understand, it happens to us all. Mom Bosses know how to discern what their customers and communities want, and to supply it. Clinging too hard to an idea that only you appreciate isn't going to help you grow your business.

Each month, I look at the top ten posts from my websites. I see what type of content my readers are engaging with. Sometimes, I scratch my head that what I thought was awesome didn't resonate. Rather than thinking my readers are idiots, I follow them where they are leading me. What have I learned? My readers don't care what celebrities are wearing. They want to see real clothes on real women. They also like wine. They like wine a lot. They don't care about the fancy sponsored events I go to; they do care about where I take my kids on vacation.

It was a mistake to write up all those event recaps. No one read them on my sites. And no one cared about the "Saturday Steals and Deals" I posted religiously for a year. My reader will pay full price for things, she shops based on quality and convenience, not necessarily price. The more I learn about her, the better I can serve her.

We listened. At Momtrends, we have developed a weekly fashion posts featuring real fashion on real moms, and we started a weekly cocktail feature. Saturday Sips is 10x more popular than steals and deals EVER was.

Get to know your customer. Let her surprise you. Let her steer you towards your next great business decision. We're just here to serve our communities and our customers. Let's say you're a designer - be sure to look at the top styles that are selling. Ask your shopper why they loved that item, then give her more of that. As a physical therapist, you should find where your top referral sources are coming from. Then spend more time fanning the flame of that referral source. There is always something to be learned at the end of the month. Use your feedback and statistics well.

Letting go can lead to bigger and better things. Dabney Lee is the founder and creative director of her eponymous company. Dabney started her stationery and paper supply business long before the triplets (yes triplets) came along 11 years ago.

Throughout her career, Dabney has used both her successes and failures as tools. "Each mistake is a different way to learn. I think about what happened, try to figure out why it happened, and what to do next time to make it a success," Dabney says.

Dabney was always curious about consumer preferences - she pays attention to what is selling and what is languishing. "When I first launched my line, I made super cute file folders that had a pattern on the outside and inside. I thought for sure we would sell through our entire stock, but they didn't sell," Dabney says. Maybe she was early to the printed office supply trend, or maybe the colors were wrong. The key is, Dabney found out there was no consumer demand, donated the folders, and moved on.

One Door Opens...

After having her three children, Dabney opened up a retail shop in DUMBO Brooklyn. The shop was colorful, whimsical, and a perfect spot to find special gifts, home décor, and the most delightful stationery. The problem was the rent. "The rents in Brooklyn have become ridiculous; it's difficult for small shops to stay open," Dabney says. While she lamented the closing of her bricks and mortar business, she didn't stop designing. She doubled down on her licensing deals with brands like Target and TJ Maxx, and focused her efforts on e-commerce. "Licensing has been my biggest success thus far. It's always a pinch me moment when I see my items in a retailer like Target!" Dabney says. If the retail shop hadn't shut, Dabney might have missed out on this new and lucrative partnership. Now Dabney says her "most popular items are cases from our tech line for Target."

Yes, it's sad that retail businesses fail, but Mom Bosses know that when one door closes, a window usually opens. "I have, absolutely, learned so much from my failures. They happen, and when they do, you pick yourself up, dust yourself off, and move forward," Dabney says.

Are You Listening?

Dabney is slightly obsessed with making her customers happy. "I am the one who is up at night worrying about whether my customers are happy." When she had her Brooklyn store, it was so easy to find out what women were touching and pondering. She met her customers on a daily basis. She learned that she must keep on top of customer feedback. "Now I stay in touch via email, Facebook, and text," Dabney says.

Don't Forget to Laugh

Dabney recalls her pre-kids days with a giggle, "I often laugh about how before I had my kids, I would complain about how busy I was. Honestly, what was I doing?" Now, the successful Mom Boss embraces her full life. "Every second of my day is scheduled to the max. I have so much more focus now than ever before. My kiddos inspire me to create and be a mama they can be proud of." Spoken like a true Mom Boss.

Chapter 14

MOM MARKETPLACE

The best business idea in the world won't do you much good if you don't have a strong community. Mom Bosses respect the power of communication and relationships. They know that a chance playground encounter could be the next investor in their brand, and the next Instagram follower might become a valuable customer.

Nurturing and cultivating community takes a ton of TLC. In fact, it's a lot like motherhood - which is good news for Mom Bosses. You've already got the skill set required.

There are three things to guide your community relations:

◊ Let your community lead

◊ Strengthen the ties that bind

◊ Listen and learn

Give Them What They Want

Al Gore may claim to have invented the internet, but Carley Roney was one of the first to harness its power to create a community. In 1996 she co-founded TheKnot.com. She teamed up with three men (one of them her husband) to create an online space for couples to plot and plan the perfect wedding. Along the way, she became a trailblazing Mom Boss.

In the middle of the hot panic of site design and soliciting early stage investors, Carley got a great little surprise - her daughter Havana. Back in 1997, Carley managed to master breastfeeding AND help raise $3 million in capital. Fortunately for her, and for The Knot's community, she never stopped to ponder if she could do it. She just did it.

Twenty years later, Carley has come up for a bit of air. Along the way, she had two more kids, saw her company go public (the company is currently valued at over $400 million), and launched two more massive internet properties - TheNest.com and TheBump.com.

Carley credits The Knot's success to two things: One, they have a unique voice. The site doesn't force-feeding traditional wedding planning to its readers. Two, the business was based on a community.

Carley preaches that a great brand is nothing without a great community. She's figured out how to grow three powerful community engines that serve The Knot - her readers, her community page managers, and her small business clients.

Let Your People Show You the Way

At the core, The Knot was there to solve a problem. It was a site for all those folks with a wedding to plan who wanted anything but the experience of flipping through a traditional bride's magazine.

Many new companies make the mistake of trying to control the brand out in the world. They try to force feed customers what they think they will want. The Knot did things differently; they started with conversations.

"Our community comes first. Clients come second," Carley says. That statement might make some investors cringe, but it's how they set themselves apart. Advertisers are sometimes bashed in the community pages, and come complaining to the sales team. The Knot won't edit those comments out of the community pages. "The only thing we edit is hate speech," Carley says.

The Knot was an early supporter of gay weddings, too. They don't discriminate. The goal is, and has always been, to help all couples navigate wedding planning and have a place to share an exciting moment in time.

All this attention to community allowed the company to sink money into building a better product (faster speeds, better interfaces) instead of spending big bucks on advertising. They didn't need a huge marketing budget; word of mouth was brings in droves of new brides and grooms.

Following the Leaders

The Knot started with a chat-based platform, where individuals can weigh in on trends they love and hate. Ground-breaking at the time, The Knot was designed to have hundreds of chats happening simultaneously. Community moderators were hired to oversee the conversations on the site. Moderators would start discussion topics, and keep things moving in productive directions. The lean team at The Knot HQ gave the moderators a lot of freedom.

"One day I came into the office and found out the moderators had named themselves the 'knotties'," Carley says. It wasn't a dream name, but rather than intervene, Carley let it ride. "The moderators had claimed a new status. They created a dynamic that was fun and inclusive." By giving her team the freedom to manage their work style, she allowed creativity to blossom.

The "knotties" felt like they were part of a movement that was larger than themselves. Carley was prescient enough to know she couldn't have hoped for a better outcome. She invested in their requests, recognizing that this powerful group of employees could be her best marketing tool. Her employees felt respected, and the readership continued to grow.

Paying Attention

Though the company may put the reader first, they also deliver exceptional value to their advertisers. They started big, and then went small. The first advertisers were Macy's, Target, etc. Once they had the technology to match the targeted ads to a local geography (for instance, if you have a catering company in Houston, your ads will be served up only to Houston couples), the Knot's sales team went about building a community of small business partners. Now, 75 percent of the advertisers on their site are small, local businesses.

"This is the community I feel most proud of," Carley says. "We are a lifeline for them to find customers and grow." They have 30,000 small business partners across the country; from photographers, to graphic designers, to DJs, these clients rely on The Knot to match them with brides and grooms. Many of the small businesses they advertise are Mom Boss businesses. "I want to empower these women to start companies," Carley says.

She takes the responsibility to provide value for their advertising dollars very seriously. "We can make or break their business," Carley says. A $1,200 yearly marketing budget for a small business owner is a huge deal. This might make or break a local florist or baker. Carley has a team to support these small entrepreneurs; they help design ads, read analytics, and target audiences. And it works. The Knot has a HUGE retention rates for advertisers, and loads of success stories.

Carley has backed off a bit from the day-to-day running of her business, and now serves as the Brand Ambassador. She devotes her resources to helping the next generation of women leaders figure out the mysteries of community building. "Listening to your customers one time a year after taking a big survey is no longer sufficient," Carley says.

YOU'VE GOT TO LISTEN EVERY DAY, AND GIVE YOUR CUSTOMERS MORE OF WHAT THEY WANT.

Rallying the Troops

Sometimes the communities Mom Bosses build are intensely personal and stronger than steel. Most people know military families make huge sacrifices to serve our country. Beyond the bravery, there's the fact that these families constantly relocate. Women that head up military families know how to grow roots fast.

While most of the moms that head military families are adept at quickly making new friends, Jen Griswold is a networker extraordinaire. This mom is a magnet of positivity and light. It no wonder she's one of the nation's top leaders of Rodan + Fields skincare.

Jen set out to be a pilot when she attended the Air Force Academy. Having met her future husband as cadets, upon graduation, she changed course and began her career as an Aircraft Maintenance Officer so they could be stationed together. A handful of years into their careers, Jen and her husband started a family....a military family. It's not easy having one spouse in the military. Two parents on active service is down-right impossible. When Jen got the opportunity, she left active duty and became a member of the Air Force Reserves.

The mom of two, was the mastermind of many moves and oversaw the family's social life. But it wasn't quite enough. "I was looking for something else, I wanted a magical six-figure, part-time job that would move with me as I moved around the country, but unfortunately it doesn't exist," says Jen.

She tapped into one of her gifts, making other women in her community feel appreciated and loved. At first, she launched a decorating business while stationed in California. Jen catered to military families and loved her work; it opened her eyes to the joy of entrepreneurism. She was hooked.

A new assignment for her husband brought her across the country from California to the Pentagon in Washington DC. She sold her decorating business and was keeping an eye out for her next opportunity. "A friend told me about Rodan + Fields, but to be honest with you at first I thought I was above it. But then I listened, really listened and I was intrigued," says Jen. Listening to her friend, she was convinced that it was the perfect time to invest her time into building a sales team to empower military spouses. She loved that Rodan +Fields was a cutting edge new company with a new model of direct sales. There were no parties, no paperwork, and no product stocking. Rodan + Fields promised to invest in developing cutting edge skincare not just fancy marketing.

Supporting Your Team

She believed in the product, loved the business model and was a smashing success. Jen attributes her achievements to being great at maintaining relationships. In the social commerce business, you get to choose who you work with. "I had a great network and I knew it, I'm good at it, most military women are," says Jen. She's cultivated friendships with each new post. "We move every two to three years. Every time I move, it enhances my business, because I collect new friends" say Jen. The key is not just collecting but giving. She's a consummate connector of people and loves sharing her entrepreneurial success with her friends.

When it comes to building out her team Jen looks for certain qualities. "I look for someone who loves people, who loves a challenge, and for someone who loves helping others," says Jen. Military moms are an exquisite fit.

Jen knew how much her peers sacrifice and knows that most of them have latent leadership skills waiting to be tapped. Instead of focusing on selling, Jen focuses on building community, or as she put it, "breeding leadership."

Her business has grown exponentially since Jen joined in 2010. She is now in the top 0.1% of Rodan + Fields consultants making a multiple six figure income. Nowadays Jen spends about 20-30 hours working each week. Her role now is to train and motivate her teammates to lead, flourish and grow. "I am leveraging what I know to help people...which is so fulfilling," say Jen.

Empowering Your Community

To date, Jen has expanded her team to over 5,000 people. While she still believes in the skincare products her team offers, she equally believes in her team's potential to lead. "These women rarely ever get told --'you're amazing.' Nobody really says that to them in their everyday lives," observes Jen. Jen spends her work hours on education; hosting training calls and managing a huge team facebook page. She also earmarks time to praise her team. It could be a shout out on social media, or a mention on a conference call. As a leader, she knows the power of well-timed praise.

Many direct sales companies provide material incentives to spur on sales. Jen has experimented with different means of motivating her sales force. There are the much-appreciated gifts of jewelry and handbags, but then she also has gifts that are career investments. She will pay for a professional headshot or a new computer. And sometimes the gift is a donation to a charity. It's always about substance in addition to style.

Giving Back to Your Community

With her success, Jen, along with her childhood friend and business partner, Jamie Petersen, have been able to spread a lot of joy in the extended military community. In fact, they gave their Rodan + Fields team the name "Team GIVE." **The acronym stands for:**

◊ Genuine

◊ Inspired

◊ Vibrant

◊ Entrepreneurs

Each season, Team GIVE selects a charity (usually related to military service) to receive a portion of their donations from increased sales. They've worked with a variety of causes, including the Knights of Heroes.

"It's not just money, but what you can do with it," Jen says. Knights of Heroes is a summer camp for kids that have lost parents to military service. Jen knows how to speak the language of her peers. Last year, Jen and the other Team GIVE leaders reached out to their team with a challenge: they asked them to sell a little more in the hopes of supporting more kids. Her team heard the call. They raised $20,000 through their fall sales, and built a new summer cabin at Knights of Heroes funded by Rodan + Fields profits.

Jen's first motivation was to serve military spouses with great skin-care products while having a flexible and rewarding career opportunity. With her bountiful financial rewards, Jen sees her Mom Boss role in a new light. She is in an even more powerful position to give back. Since the beginning, Jen has given generously to Lift Fund. Lift Fund is a micro-lending resource, providing credit and services to small businesses and entrepreneurs who do not have access to traditional loans. Jen is focused on getting micro-funding into the hands of military spouses who want to launch small businesses. "The whole underlying theme of our team is to succeed so we can give back," Jen says.

Service With a Smile

In direct sales, you've got to ask yourself how you will serve your community. Without a connection and a passion, you'll likely join the ranks of women who drop out. In fact, over half of the women who start a direct sales position this year will quit.

> **IF YOU DON'T HAVE A SENSE OF SERVICE TO YOUR COMMUNITY, YOU WON'T HAVE LASTING SUCCESS.**

Caroline Oliver is relatively new to the Mom Boss world. She joined the Arbonne skincare sales team because she believed in the product, and liked the flexibility. The Connecticut-based mom cites her expanded social network as the best perk of the business.

"I am a very social person, and I found out that, ultimately, I didn't want to be a lawyer. This is a profession that is much more suited to my personality and interests," Caroline says. Mom Bosses that venture into direct sales almost always are the ones who adore meeting new people. They are also likely to be interested in serving their community. "Whether it is making better choices in terms of personal care products, or having the opportunity to help them make a life changing income, I want to help," Caroline says.

Caroline picked Arbonne because "there is a lot of emphasis on being authentic." In Arbonne's structure, it is very important to have a strong client base as well as a strong team for the most success. When you feel your business is an extension of yourself, it's easy to market to your friends. There's a natural opening to integrate your passion for your career into the communities where you belong, but it must come from a place of authenticity.

Listening and Learning

Alyson Seligman started her online ventures after a serious health scare; she was diagnosed with a rare neuro condition which changed her life. On her journey back to health, she started blogging on her site, TheAverageGirlsGuide.com. Her site has a hugely devoted following who love her mix of career, fashion, and family. She serves up great content that keeps her community of readers coming back for more.

Part of the reason Alyson has been successful in a very crowded blogosphere space is that she listens closely to her community. She tracks blog posts that perform well - like her real world style picks - and gives her audience more of what they want.

In time, word about Alyson's social media skills got out. Friends and businesses in her South Florida area admired her ability to navigate the new media world, and started asking Alyson for consulting help. She launched the SBS Agency to fill a need. It's a PR agency and a creative agency rolled into one. After starting her career in PR, it all came back full circle. Now she has a flexible work life and creates her own opportunities.

One of Alyson's tips for Mom Bosses is this: Don't neglect your relationships. When it comes to social media, you've got to tend to your accounts even when you're not actively looking to promote something. "There's always value in showcasing to the world the best version of yourself. Don't think about it as sales, think about it as relationship building. You'll be pleasantly surprised over the long-term how much value it adds," Alyson says.

Think about every post before you share it with your community. "Brand yourself. Is the person you're showing on your social channels the person you strive to be and want to present to the world?" Alyson says. She advises you to develop cohesive content so your brand fans know what to expect.

Now, six years into her agency, Alyson is once again taking stock. She's listening to her community and herself to figure out what's next. "I'm having a lot of honest moments, and I'm excited for what's to come," Alyson says.

Wondering what's next for your Mom Boss brand?

LISTEN TO YOUR COMMUNITY, AND THEY WILL TELL YOU WHERE TO GO.

Chapter 15

GETTING IT DONE

I t's time to figure out what your work life will look like. Mom Bosses know how to make that 25th hour in the day appear. Moms are already masters of efficiency. Remember your life before kids – you thought you were so busy? Ha! Somehow, you managed to add children into the mix. The same will hold true for your work.

Warning: This is the part where I tell you it isn't always pretty. 61 percent of mothers with children under six are working. 100 percent of the Mom Bosses in that group long for more sleep. From speaking to more than 50 Mom Bosses for this book, here's what I learned:

◊ **We plan meals**

◊ **We write to-do lists**

◊ **We rely on help at home**

◊ **We multitask**

We use short snippets of time to accomplish what needs to get done. 50 percent of this book was written on my phone: during subway rides as I traveled between meetings, sitting outside of piano lessons, and waiting at the orthodontist's office. Our top two resources are time and money; time to protect these resources.

Make Your Own Safety Net

Farnoosh Torabi built a freelance career long before losing her job at a traditional publishing house. She spent a few lucrative and productive years writing books and building up her personal brand as a financial expert. She wrote her first book, **You're So Money**, while still working her day job. By the time Farnoosh's baby arrived, she had been supporting herself for years, and was fully prepped for life as a Mom Boss.

Farnoosh advises all Mom Bosses to be realistic about the first year of the business. Before you start spending money (and definitely before you quit your job) have a business plan. "It's like writing a book, the longer you spend working on the table of contents, the easier the book is to write," Farnoosh says. That doesn't mean venturing into analysis paralysis territory. It means thinking about where your profits will come from, how long it will take you to turn a profit, and how you will measure your success. "Learn what you need for the next six months," Farnoosh advises.

If you are leaving a well-paying job, you are probably not going to replace the income you were making before you became an entrepreneur. Factor in the loss to your family income before you leave your company.

You'll need to budget for the start-up expenses, but remember there are some baked-in savings. By working from home for a few months, you can back the savings into getting your business off the ground. If you are working from home, you'll save on commuting and childcare (though you probably will want to have some sort of childcare in place to be most productive). You'll also be able to eat at home, and might not have to spend as much on your work wardrobe.

Invest in Your Success

"The more you invest in systems early on, the more time you will allow yourself to be a visionary for your brand," Farnoosh says. Having systems in place will allow you to get back to the exciting portion of the business.

One way to find more time in your day is to hire a virtual assistant to do mundane tasks like invoicing, or managing a database. Hiring others can help you avoid costly mistakes. While you may think you can master payroll on your own, the $150 service fee you pay ADP to manage your payroll might protect you from Uncle Sam's wrath if you fail to pay state unemployment taxes.

Keep the Cash Flowing

Farnoosh says that women are much more hesitant than men to ask for deals. Farnoosh advises Mom Bosses to negotiate with suppliers, consultants, and freelancers. Even asking for a simple 10 percent reduction in fees can add up. Remember, every penny you save on expenses is almost as important as your income. Negotiating deals will make your margins much, much healthier.

Don't be shy about collecting your payments.

1. Clearly set the expectations. Sign a contract or have an email agreement. You want a paper trail.

2. Promptly Invoice, and make many payment options available.

3. Send scheduled reminders. At Momtrends, we send a reminder email when an invoice is overdue by a week. A second reminder goes out at two weeks. At three weeks, we call and email. By four weeks, we get legal advice.

Ask for Help at Home

When Farnosh went back to work after the birth of her son, she got a nanny and moved her office to a We Work space. She had support and an environment conducive to work. But even with help, she found it was incredibly hard to get all of her work done before the nanny left at 4 p.m. Farnoosh was overwhelmed.

Rather than being a martyr, Farnoosh asked for help. Her husband wanted to contribute. He was able to meet the nanny at 4 p.m. a few days a week so that Farnoosh could finish off work projects. Once they were splitting the 4 p.m. change duty, "there was a seismic shift in my happiness and identity," Farnoosh says. There's no need to be a super mom.

Remember ladies, most of our significant others want to help. For me, the writing of this book posed a significant problem. I didn't know where I wasn't going to find the extra six to eight hours a week I needed to interview all the amazing moms featured in this book and get down to writing. Mr. Momtrends came to the rescue. He started preparing breakfast for the girls and taking them to school four days a week. This helped me recover about an hour of work a day (the rest, sadly, came out of my sleep savings bank).

Asking for help and setting limits will prevent Mom Boss burnout. After all, many of us gravitated towards entrepreneurship because of its freedom and creativity. Mom Bosses have to be careful not to let the business consume them. You have to work to create the space you need to be creative and best serve your clients and customers.

Before becoming a Mom Boss, Christine Koh was a brain scientist. She spent a decade in academia studying brain behavior and cognitive processes, with a specialized focus on music and the brain.

When Christine recognized her passions were shifting, she left academia to pursue family and creative endeavors. Two notable things happened; she became a mom, and her father died. "These two things very much made me question what I was doing – I really felt that if I was going to work and spend so many hours away from the people I loved, I needed to be passionate about what I was doing," Christine says. The hours away from home coincided with the growth of her website (BostonMamas.com), and she jumped into Mom Boss life.

While she doesn't work less hard in her creative pursuits (she also co-authored **Minimalist Parenting**, co-hosts the Edit Your Life podcast, and is the creative director at Women Online), she does have the ability to make her own schedule. She's devoted her Mom Boss career to helping folks get rid of clutter - visually and spiritually.

A Space of One's Own

Many Mom Bosses like Christine work from home - it's essential to carve out a dedicate work space. Christine designed a home office that's "clean and minimal, with a glam edge." You want an area that you can call off-limits to the rest of the family; even if it's a work space in the kitchen, carve it out as your own, personalize it, and claim it like a Mom Boss. It's not about the size of the office; it's about how you feel when you work.

The Rhythm of the Day

Mom Bosses have the luxury of setting their office hours. Christine gets her two kids off to school, and then starts her day with a run or yoga. From there, Christine jumps into work mode - writing, making client calls, fielding emails. Every day looks a little different when it comes to work projects, but one thing remains the same - a little transition time at the end of the day. Since Christine doesn't have the benefit of a commute to shift from work mode to family mode, she makes one. She'll pencil in 30 minutes at the end of the day for meditation before the kids get home, or she'll plan to walk instead of drive to go pick up her little one from pre-K. "Carving out the time to let my brain unwind after a busy day is critical to me being more present (and more fun!) with my family," Christine says.

Where does she find the time for this self care? She's passionate about lifestyle editing. "When you're a Mom Boss, you have a million people and things pulling at you in different directions, and that makes it more important than ever to really think and act with care and intention," Christine says. We have to be choosy. That means saying no to things so that we can build in empty space on the calendar. Christine says, "We all deserve to live a well curated life, and have permission to do less of what we don't want to do so we have more room for awesome."

Mom Boss Tip

Christine advises inserting a short midday break to do something not digital or work related. For her, it's picking up her guitar and strumming for a few minutes.

"For me, success is about being great in your work, but it's also very much about making self-care a priority, nurturing your relationships (as a parent, partner, friend, etc.), and operating with generosity and kindness in the world," Christine says. A small and purposeful business may bring you ten-fold the rewards of a six-figure corporate job with six-figure stress.

No two Mom Bosses have the same work/life balance. In fact, typical work days don't exist for Mom Bosses. When it comes to scheduling, you have to set up hours that work for you. At Momtrends we hold weekly sales meetings at 11am every Wednesday;

I've learned that to be successful, my team needs consistency. I don't set many meetings on the calendar (in general I think they are a HUGE waste of time), so the ones I put on the calendar have to stick.

Make the Most of Every Minute

Robyn Carter is the founder and CEO of Jump Rope Innovation, a trends and innovation consultancy. She began her career in the ad agency world, working on a host of iconic brands, including Red Stripe and Maxwell House. As a Mom Boss, she still gets to work with top brands - she just does it while based from home.

Today, Robyn helps lead top tier clients such as Unilever, Hershey's, and Campbell's develop new products and strategize to better serve their customers. Being a Mom Boss doesn't mean she's less in demand - it means she must master the art of prioritizing. And it's never easy.

"I hold my breath and say a little prayer any time something that is important comes up at the last minute. Usually if it's important, I can make it work," Robyn says.

The struggle is real for Robyn. "I can remember my daughter being two or three years old, standing at her play kitchen, looking over at me at my desk, and saying, 'Mommy, come play with me,' and I couldn't," Robyn says. Robyn's daughter learned to play alone beside Robyn's desk. Instead of giving into the Mom Guilt, Robyn talks with her family about why her work matters.

"It still breaks my heart to see her in my mind's eye, turning to me and asking me to play - and thinking that she learned to play on her own because I was too busy to play with her," Robyn says. But then she remembers that she's contributing financially to her family's needs and giving her daughter a powerful role model.

The upside is, all our efforts matter. "I get to show my daughter that someday she can have kids, love them, be there for them, and still have something that is hers. - Something that is about her as a person, not as a mommy – and she can feel good about that," Robyn says.

Mom Boss Tip

Schedule overlapping afterschool activitie s for your kids – they might not both love soccer, but if you can swing two practices on the same field at the same time, consider it a win.

What does a Mom Boss do to get the job done? She gets creative. "In a pinch, when my kids were younger and more likely to go rogue if uncontained, I might put on a movie in the car, with them buckled into their car seats, and stand outside the car to take a call," Robyn says.

Finally, learn how to say no. It's so hard when you are launching your business to turn down opportunities. But you've got to be protective of your resources – time and money. Never lose sight that you started this all to be more present for your family. Robyn says, "I say no to projects that are truly outside my wheelhouse, or that are really not intrinsically interesting; projects that don't help me to grow in a direction that makes strategic sense for my business. I'm paying for those opportunities with time. Those sorts of projects take away from time I could be spending with my kids, without much meaningful reward."

Mom Bosses often get misunderstood by other parents and teachers. While we might work from home or for ourselves, we can't always swing last-minute field trip duty and work just as many hours as the parents marching off to more traditional jobs. We also stress out about last-minute school projects and end of year performances that seem to magically appear on the calendar.

You take on a big job when you become a Mom Boss. There are two things you will pour into your new business: your time, and your money. You want to make sure you use both of them well.

Many nights I am up until 1 or 2 a.m., finishing off a writing project or campaign. Daytime is for photography, meetings, exercise, and family. I'm on top of the big stuff: recitals, doctors appointments, chorus performances, but I have had to let some of the little things go. I call it benign neglect. I also call it a gift. The girls have had to become more responsible than some of their peers since I simply can't be stretched any farther. They do school projects 95 percent on their own (I'll order a last-minute costume from Amazon, but I'm not hand-sewing pilgrim dress or hand-baking cupcakes). Mom Bosses have to master the art of letting go.

Chapter 16

GRATITUDE

Since it's such a huge part of the Mom Boss business model, it's only fitting that the last chapter is about gratitude—for those who support us. Clearly you're going to need a lot of passion to pull this off, don't neglect the people and relationships (both personal and professional) along the road towards financial success.

Galit Lebow is the Co-CEO & Co-Founder of Foodstirs, a kid-centric baking brand. No stranger to startups, before Foodstirs, Galit co-founded a PR firm called Ink Public Relations. For 10 years, Galit delivered innovative brand awareness campaigns for her clients. It's no surprise she's bringing a fresh take on the baking aisle—combining quality ingredients, creative packaging with a spirit of play.

Early on, Galit decided to seek out co-founders for this company. "We three co-founders each have a special skill that we bring to Foodstirs. For me, having founded and run a business before - I play the Operator. Gia (Russo) with her background in product development, is our Innovator, and Sarah Michelle (Gellar) is our Master Craftswoman helping shape the Foodstirs consumer experience," says Galit.

According to Bloomberg, 8 out of 10 entrepreneurs who start businesses fail within the first 18 months. Foodstirs thrived where other start-ups floundered. The difference was the passion and the partnerships. Galt credits here partners with being quick to adapt when something may not be working as expected.

It doesn't hurt having the built-in fan base of celebrity co-founder, Sarah Michelle Gellar. While celebrity may get you attention, it's not going to create brand fans. That has to come from having a product that serves its customers well.

Sharing is Caring

The business model is based on sharing. Parents want to share time with their children in meaningful ways. Kitchen playdates are a tremendous source of fun and a great chance to bond over baking. But gathering the ingredients, finding the recipes and making it actually fun, not a chore...that's the challenge.

Not surprisingly, many Mom Bosses are looking to build brands and experiences that enhance or improve life. Yes, these women want to make money, but they also want to put more goodness out into the universe. Galit's company isn't a food company, it's an experience company. The goal is to get families back into the kitchen, experimenting, playing and making joyful messes. Foodstirs takes the hard work out of the equation by sourcing high-quality ingredients and providing step-by-step instructions. In addition to the cooking project, there's always an element of crafting or play involved in every Foodstirs kit.

Galit feels exceptionally lucky to be living her passion while solving problems for other busy parents. "I'm passionate about what were are doing to create richer family experiences which makes it all worth it," says Galit.

Galit and her team take it very seriously that their customers are inviting her brand into an intimate homespace—the kitchen. Hours and hours of research go into each new product like the Ombre Pancake Kit. Galit studies Pinterest trends dreaming up new ways to delight and surprise her customers. "Pinterest actually fueled the idea of the baking kits. We wanted to bring consumers an experience that they could actually execute," says Galit. Foodstirs takes inspiration from fancy cooking shows, magazines and social media and breaks it down to a doable project. Success is almost guaranteed.

We 'like" You

Foodstirs "gets" the power of the likeability. Galit and her team do a remarkable job of including the community in their marketing efforts. Savvy brands like Foodstirs encourage customers to share their experience on social media platforms. When fans share a share a completed backing project, they tag (or call out with a specific mention) Foodstirs. Galit's social media team is incredibly responsive. And Sarah Michelle gets involved too. Boy do the fans go bananas when Sarah Michelle makes a comment directly on a fan's accoun—the loyalty factor is HUGE!

NEVER UNDERESTIMATE THE POWER OF A KIND WORD AND ENCOURAGEMENT TO BUILD CUSTOMER LOYALTY.

The "box" experience has grown substantially in the last decade. Foodstirs stands out for what they do with the feedback they get. Because sometimes the cookie literally crumbles and a recipe goes awry. Rather than ignore the issues, Galit tackles them head on. "I do not fear failure. I evaluate for the learning opportunity and then quickly adapt, innovate, and overcome so our business can stay on track and grow," says Galit.

Growth Through Gratitude

Kimberly Inskeep is the President & Chief Culture Officer at cabi. In 2002 she teamed up with Head Designer, Carol Anderson, to help create a new retail sales model. They wanted to leave the traditional wholesale model of selling clothes and create a different culture with a different shopping experience. Carol and Kimberly brought in ten additional women (the cabi "Founders") to be the first sales force. Together, they reshaped what it meant to shop for clothes.

Now 15 years later cabi is the "largest apparel company without brick and mortar stores." They empower a team of home-based stylists to sell clothing through "Fashion Experiences"—home shows where trained cabi stylists present the season's trends. Each stylist is more than a salesperson, she's there to help women put together a customized wardrobe. All in, cabi has more than 3500 stylists who sell millions of dollars of clothing and jewelry each season, it's not unusual for a cabi stylist to earn well over $30,000 a year while working from home around her family's schedule.

Cabi asks for a much larger investment of money from their team members. Unlike direct sales companies, cabi isn't for those who dabble. They've set themselves apart with their product and but the secret sauce is really the training and the support system.

To make sure they are attracting women who will approach the business opportunities purposefully, they require an initial entry investment of about $2500 (this goes towards a season's worth of clothing samples that the stylist will be able to sell at the end of the season). In comparison, direct sales companies, require new members to put much less skin in the game. When you are selling candles, skincare or vitamins you can easily get your foot in the door for $99. With this businesses you aren't out much. If you change your mind a few months later, not big deal. Cabi does things differently. They want women thinking long-term and strategically.

That's not where the differences end. Cabi eschews the direct sales model in favor of a framework that is all about support and growth. Kimberly and her executive team are there to create success stories by leading with generosity and providing support.

According to Kimberly, 20% of people who enter direct sales remain in place a year later. Clearly cabi isn't a direct sales model. Cabi has an 85% retention rate—being picky about who they partner with pays off. For both brand and stylist, there needs to be a lot of thought, research and care done before writing the check and joining.

Choose Your Partners Wisely

"When a woman decides to start a cabi business she has to go through a decision making process," says Kimberly. Most of the training focus at cabi is on teaching women how to become stylists and develop long term relationships. Kimberly says, "First and foremost it's about giving women a different shopping experience." Women who sell cabi have to gain the trust and respect of their clientele to succeed and that can only happen if they adopt a sense of gratitude and generosity.

"When we started the company with our ten founders, we made sure that our brand was based on gratitude," says Kimberly. Gift giving is a common practice in the corporate culture. When the first few hundred stylists began, Kimberly and her team lavished them with handwritten notes and gifts. "In the early days I wrote a thousands of handwritten notes to all our stylists and today continue to reach out whether to acknowledge achievement, a loss of a loved one, or personal illness," says Kimberly. She intentionally paid attention to small details–her management style is high touch and in turn she inspires those around her to create equally intimate relationships with their cabi customers.

Under "gifting," . . . When the first few hundred stylists began (not just the first 10), we lavished them with handwritten notes and gifts. "In the early days I wrote a thousands of hand written notes to all our stylists and today continue to reach out whether to acknowledge achievement, a loss of a loved one, or personal illness," says Kimberly

"In the early days I wrote a thousand hand written notes to all our consultants before our biannual meeting," says Kimberly. The brand just expanded into Canada and the UK, so while all those personal notes might not be possible at each meeting, Kimberly still pens thank you notes to top sellers and says, "I still believe in the spirit of gratitude."

Kimberly has a college-age daughter who grew up watching her mom grow a business. Her daughter was able to witness first-hand that one can lead with generosity and be very successful. "I believe when you give, it will come back to you ten-fold," says Kimberly.

Doing Well to do Good

The financial model has made a lot of cabi consultants and the management team wealthy. As a brand, they believe in paying it forward. Cabi doesn't just write the occasional check to a feel-good charity. From the start, they've found partners. "We started the brand with a belief in giving back," says Kimberly. In 2005 cabi formally created the Heart of cabi Foundation. To date, the foundation has given away more than $45 million worth of clothing and funded more than 8,000 microloans for small businesses (which translates into over 40,000 new jobs). "When you have been given much, you have a responsibility to be a good steward," says Kimberly.

While new companies might not be able to contribute on that scope, a Mom Boss business of any size can find a way to give back. Kimberly says, "Look around and see who is in need." If you're a baker, you can give your goods to a charity partner, if you're selling baby gear you can earmark a portion of each season's samples to a clothing drive.

MAKE GIVING BACK PART OF YOUR BUSINESS PLAN.

Creative Ways to Show Your Gratitude:

Whether your brand is big or small, you can practice the art of generosity.

Gifting: At cabi, it is a common practice is for a sales associate to bring a gift to each hostess that she teams up with for a styling event. After the event, the cabi management team will often send a bouquet of flowers to the hostess at parties that have large sales total.

Write a note: Nothing is more cost-effective than a handwritten note on pretty stationery. Emails are nice, but a personally penned message means twice as much.

Referrals: The "word of mom" is worth gold. Think about how you can use your network to help others. If your dentist is one of your top bakery customers, be sure to refer her practice to friends. Shop and support your customers.

Say Thank You: Praise your work family and your clients often and be specific with your praise.

For example:

Don't just say: "Nice job on that presentation."

Instead try: "I was so impressed by the visual continuity of your deck, they way you worked in instagram examples really helped me understand the power of using the right filter".

175

Do your best to put others in the spotlight. When one of our editors writes an especially brilliant post, I link to it on my personal Facebook page with a note calling attention to the writer and thanking her for the efforts.

Make a Donation: Show your brand fans and work family that you care about what THEY care about. When a member of our extended community of bloggers is raising money for a charity, I always like to make a small donation. I want to show our blogging peers that I am listening and paying attention.

The more you show you are paying attention and care about the needs of your community the more your company will flourish.

No Mom Boss is an Island

Even if you have a small freelance business, there are always folks that have helped lift you up and supported you somewhere along your entrepreneurial journey. To be sure, even entrepreneurs like Jessica Alba have some rough days and need a 1am pep talk.

For many an Mom Boss, there's a spouse or partner doing a lot of cheering from the sidelines. And for some, they lasso their partners into the dream. Ready or not, they come along for the ride.

In 2009 Ellen Allen started a lifestyle brand that spoke to her. She saw a need for a great, well-priced bag that fit her coastal chic aesthetic, so with tremendous support from her husband she started designing and producing her eponymous bags. She started with three bodies of handbags and a big dream. The bags were a hit. Morning shows and glossy magazines sung her praises and orders started rolling in.

Mom Boss life is rarely moves along one trajectory. Like most entrepreneurs, Ellen Allen the brand has had some ups and downs. Along the way, Ellen Allen the mom says her husband Don Allen, has never wavered in his support or asked to get off the merry-go-round.

It's so much easier (and a lot more fun) to know your spouse has your back. "Don is amazing. "How many Dads do you know that will happily keep an eye on the kids while you're in China for 10 days negotiating with factories!" says Ellen. She sings his praises and encourages Mom Bosses to manage their work/life balance with respect and honesty.

Our Motto is "it's fine, it's fine, keep going," says Ellen. With two kids, a mortgage and college looming, they never lose hope or perspective and most importantly their sense of humor.

Ellen recalled the early days of her brand and it sounded a lot like falling in love. "In the beginning it's the most exciting you've ever done," says Ellen. With all the excitement, it's only natural that your enthusiasm gushes over into your homelife. With the wins, it's awesome to celebrate with your partner. And when things go wrong, like having a $50,000 handbag delivery arrive from China with faulty handles, well, you want to share that too.

Don stood by Ellen when Ellen Allen the company faced a huge financial risk. When a shipment of damaged bags arrived from China, Ellen knew she couldn't put her name on the bags and sell them. She couldn't do that to the brand she loved.

This could have been the end of the story for the brand. The question was, "what's next?" Was it time for Ellen to go back to teaching and abandon ship. Not yet. Thankfully for her brand fans, Don and Ellen operate from a place of "unconditional hope."

Ellen shares, "Unconditional Hope must be ever present, even when all evidence is to the contrary. There are a ton of sacrifices that are made daily– the love and support Don Allen gives make it all possible," says Ellen.

With Don cheering her on, Ellen has started the hunt for a domestic manufacturer and has found a business partner to share some of the financial risks. Due to the China fiasco, Ellen Allen bags have delivered little revenue for two and half years. "There are so many ups and downs that occur, if Don Allen was not on board with my dreams and vision, there would be no EAA," says Ellen. But Ellen isn't done hoping for better days ahead. "The truth is that every day I don't get run over by the proverbial bus of life is a good day. Every day that I don't end up with a sick kid, coffee down my shirt, or my husband doesn't inform me that he's considering a transfer to Kenosha, WI, is a good day. I celebrate these days. I go to bed at night and think: "That was a good day'," says Ellen

Marriage Therapy For Mom Bosses

Be clear with the numbers: Unless you're independently wealthy, you need to be open and honest about how much you're willing to risk on your new business. Communicate your business plan with your spouse and provide monthly updates to advise on the status of the business. You need to agree on a investment amount that you can both live with. And most of all: don't hide the losses!

Clarify The Roles: Maybe your spouse is an unofficial advisor or maybe an official officer of the business, be clear about how much input you want to have. No fair complaining about bad advice if you go looking for it time and again. Set some framework for how involved your spouse will be,

Power Down: If you work from home there's a risk that Mom Boss life, like kudzu, can invade your home. Set family and couple time aside where you are offline and focus on each other. Mr.Mom-trends and I have a long-standing date night on Thursdays (10 years and counting!). We hire a sitter, and for the most part, avoid talking about kids stuff and work stuff. Romance doesn't happen by accident.

It's Not All About You: Don't let your Mom Boss life suck all the oxygen from the room. Yes, it's incredibly exciting, and scary and frustrating, but your war stories can get old to even the most sup-portive spouse. Remember to ask your partner how his or her day was and then take an interest in what they have going on too.

Say Thank You: As Ellen says, "Whether you want to or not, your partner is there with you in this journey and taking a big risk with you." Remember to be gracious.

I'm eternally grateful that my husband carried the burden of providing for our family during our start up years. While he didn't invest money in my business, he did give me the financial freedom to try this. I went from earning more than $200,000 a year at Ralph Lauren to making about $25,000 my first year as a freelance writer. Thanks to his hard work, I had the time and space to create a million-dollar brand that now contributes in meaningful ways to our family economics. I know I'm incredibly lucky and Mom Bosses should always respect those who helped along the way.

Most of us started this because of family, and they are our beacon—calling us to bed at 2am and reminding us that a Friday night dance party to Taylor Swift or a date night where we talk about anything but business is almost always a good idea. So now we give thanks, power off and get ready for the next day of Mom Boss life.

Footnotes

*footnote #1: http://www.catalyst.org/knowledge/women-ceos-sp-500

*footnote #2: http://www.theatlantic.com/sexes/a rchive/2013/04/why-43-of-women-with-children-leave-their-jobs-and-how-to-get-them-back/275134/

*footnote #3: http://techcrunch.com/2015/05/26/female-founders-on-an-upward-trend-according-to-crunchbase/

+http://www.theguardian.com/media-network/2015/aug/06/women-entrepreneurs-venture-capital-funding-tech-startups

+ https://www.rodanandfields.com/images/Achives/RF-Income-Disclosure-Statement.pdf

ACKNOWLEDGEMENTS

Thirteen years ago I bungee jumped off the Kawarau Bridge (141 feet!) in New Zealand. Jumping with me was Mr. Momtrends, the love of my life. While it's not a bridge, this book was another tremendous leap and once again he's at my side. Not one for shout outs on social media, he supports me behind the scenes. Mr. Momtrends picked up more family responsibilities to allow me to write and never grumbled about my late-night work sessions. We leap together, always looking for adventure and always cheering each other on. He reminds me to never settle for good if greatness is within my grasp.

My daughters have been fascinated by this book. I'm grateful by their inquisitive nature and their boundless enthusiasm for my work. I'm lucky that they remind me to unplug and slow down to notice ladybugs. It's for them that I created this exceptional work life and I count my blessings every day to have a business where I can be intimately involved watching them grow.

Some of us are lucky to have entrepreneurism in our blood. I was fortunate to grow up in a home full of the startup spirit. My Mom and Dad were my first entrepreneurial role models. They taught me so much about hard work, determination and caring deeply about employees. Thank you both for being such fantastic cheerleaders for me every step of the way.

To my team at Momtrends, I am inspired by your ideas big and small. You all make it fun to pop online every day and I'm so proud of the company we've built and the opportunities we've created for moms to thrive. A special thanks to Sherri and Brooke for always saying "why not" to all my big dreams. I love you both very much.

I couldn't have asked for a better first book experience. How lucky that Mango Publishing trusted me to write the book I didn't know I had inside me. My editing partner, Hugo (who is lovely, but most certainly NOT a Mom Boss), gets kudos for patiently wading through each chapter and keeping me on course all the while making this process fun.

And finally a big thanks to the Momtrends community. Without you there's no blog, book or business. Every time you swing by and time to spend time with our brand I feel honored. Our mission has always been to inspire you to be your best, and maybe this book will inspire some of you to jump. Be sure to bring me along on your Mom Boss journey.

Tag your social media posts #MomBoss and I'll find you.

AUTHOR BIO

Every mom needs a BFF. Momtrends fits that role beautifully.
Nicole Feliciano, Founder and CEO, left her role as an executive at
Ralph Lauren to launch the Momtrends blog in 2007. Since then,
Momtrends has grown into a boutique media brand that provides
the latest news on things trendy and cool for moms. Each month
more than 500,000 moms check in with Momtrends looking for the
scoop on what's fresh, pretty and purposeful.

CPSIA information can be obtained
at www.ICGtesting.com
Printed in the USA
BVOW10s2326060816

457898BV00003B/5/P